INSPIRATIONAL STORIES
of SALVATION

BY DOUG BATCHELOR

amazingfacts.org

Published by
Amazing Facts, Inc.
PO Box 1058
Roseville, CA 95678-8058
800-538-7275

Cover Art
Phil McKay

Cover Design
Eric Smalling

Text Layout
Greg Solie • Altamont Graphics

ISBN: 978-1-58019-634-5

Table of Contents

Introduction

As a boy, I once tied a towel—pretending it was a long, flowing cape—around my neck and then jumped off a roof. Why? I wanted to be like my hero Superman. (I didn't get hurt, but I don't recommend anyone else trying it.)

Someone once said, "Choose your teachers carefully, for you will become just like them." The Bible affirms this when it says, "We all, with unveiled face, beholding as in a mirror the glory of the Lord, are being transformed into the same image from glory to glory" (2 Corinthians 3:18). That's why people need good heroes; we will eventually imitate the ones we look up to and, over time, we gradually become like them. (Unless, of course, they have super powers.)

According to the dictionary, a hero is a person distinguished by his or her courage or ability, admired for brave deeds, sacrifices, or noble qualities. Unfortunately these days, multitudes of people admire the wrong heroes: strong athletes, pop singers, or glamorous actors whose personal lives are often exposed for violence, cheating, drug abuse, and other immorality. This is not new; we know that the crowd will typically choose Barabbas over Jesus.

There is a serious shortage today of godly role models for people. Perhaps it's about time we flip off the TV and open our Bibles to behold the lives of some worthy role models who point us heavenward.

One reason I feel so strongly about spending time with Bible heroes is because I know that their lives were transformed when they looked to God for hope and strength. Indeed, the great heroes of faith ultimately point us to the only one who deserves every ounce of our adoration, Jesus Christ.

All of the talk about revival in the church will remain nothing more than talk if we continue to be enamored by the fallen heroes of the world. The apostle Paul got it right when he wrote, "Therefore we also, since we are surrounded by so great a cloud of witnesses, let us lay aside every weight, and the sin which so easily ensnares us, and let us run with endurance the race that is set before us, looking unto Jesus" (Hebrews 12:1, 2).

A Bible hero is a witness who helps us fix our eyes on Christ so that our lives will be changed. As you read through this devotional workbook, it's my prayer and my hope that this collection of biblical heroes will inspire you to follow the greatest hero of faith, Jesus Christ, that much more closely.

Pastor Doug Batchelor
President, Amazing Facts

Chapter 1
Broken Chains

Bible Hero: The Demoniac of Decapolis

Champion Text: "[Jesus] said to him, 'Go home to your friends, and tell them what great things the Lord has done for you, and how He has had compassion on you'" (Mark 5:19).

Victorious Message: Anyone, no matter how shackled by the chains of sin, can be set free.

As Jesus and His disciples were crossing the Sea of Galilee one evening, they encountered a severe storm. It must have been a terrible tempest. When experienced sailors and fishermen fear for their lives out at sea, you know it's serious.

Indeed, as a pilot I'm not usually troubled by turbulence. When a plane bounces around, I've seen passengers around me get a little nervous. But when the experienced crew of the aircraft gets worried, then you know you're experiencing *real* turbulence. This once happened to me when I was traveling to Australia across the Pacific. People were standing in line at the restroom when the aircraft was violently jarred by unexpected turbulence. The flight attendant shouted to the passengers, "Sit down!" When people started walking back to their seats, she shouted, "No! Sit on the floor, now!" When a panicked flight attendant tells you to sit on the floor, you know you're in something very serious.

When the squall hit the disciples' boat, these seasoned fishermen cried out for their lives. Water swamped their vessel, and they thought they were all going to die. Yet when lightning flashed, they noticed Jesus, curled up in exhaustion, sleeping in the back of the boat on top of some nets and tackling. They shook Him and shouted, "Teacher, do You not care that we are perishing?" (Mark 4:38).

Jesus woke up and calmly took in the situation. Then He stood and, while holding onto the mast with one hand, stretched out His other hand and said to the raging elements, "Shalom." Instantly the storm stopped. It was so quiet, you couldn't have felt even a stir on the hair of your arm. The waves flattened out, and the water was as glassy as a millpond.

Notice how the Bible next describes the disciples. "They were afraid, and marveled, saying to one another, 'Who can this be? For He commands even the winds and water, and they obey Him!' " (Luke 8:25).

With this experience still fresh in their minds, Jesus directed them to row to the southeastern shore of Galilee to a region called Decapolis. It was a Greco-Roman area inhabited by Hellenistic pagans and pig farmers.

As the sun began to illuminate the eastern sky, the tired disciples saw tombstones silhouetted against the hillside. They pulled the boat up onto the beach and climbed out. Perhaps they began gathering driftwood to build a fire to dry out their wet clothes. I can picture one of the disciples pausing to sniff the wind and wonder aloud, "What is that smell?"

Another disciple might have pointed up the hillside and said, "It's probably those pigs."

The first disciple replied, "No, I've smelled pigs. That isn't pigs."

Suddenly, they all heard a bloodcurdling shriek. Running out from among the tombs came a creature that resembled something like Bigfoot. His long hair was matted, his eyes were glaring, and his mouth was snarling and foaming with saliva. He charged directly toward them, intent on tearing them all apart with his bare hands. Dragging from his ankles and wrists were shattered remnants of chains and shackles. A manacle also hung around his neck, and he was naked. His body was covered with self-inflicted cuts and wounds.

I don't imagine the disciples' first thoughts were, "Praise the Lord! Here's a wonderful opportunity to share Jesus with somebody." I think they dropped their driftwood and ran as fast as they could back to the boat. Their nerves were already frayed. They had been terrified in the storm, and now they were even more frightened. Can you picture them diving into the boat and paddling with all their might away from the shore? They probably could have pulled someone on water skis, they rowed so fast.

At some point, one of them did a head count and noticed someone was missing. As they turned their eyes back to the shore, they saw Jesus. He stood unmoved before the raving lunatic, who was, to their unbelieving eyes, kneeling at His feet. Jesus boldly asked the demon, who was speaking through the man, "What is your name?"

The demon responded, "Legion," since many demons had entered this captive of Satan. (A Roman legion of soldiers could have as many as 6,000 people!) This man was filled with devils. "And they begged Him that He would not command them to go out into the abyss" (Luke 8:31). The Greek word for abyss is *abussos* and means "out into the deep" and "the nothingness." It's the same word found in Revelation 20:1, the "bottomless pit" where all demons will someday be cast. "Now a herd of many swine was feeding there on the mountain. So they begged Him that He would permit them to enter them. And He permitted them" (verse 32).

The Story of Salvation

Let's think about the deeper meaning of this story. The messages of Scripture are not just interesting reading, and Bible events like this one paint us a fascinating picture of salvation. You see, Jesus crossed a stormy sea when He came to our world to bring peace to people lost in sin and turmoil. Look closely at this demoniac: He lived among the dead, he was unclean, and he was surrounded by pigs—unclean animals. He was also naked, covered with scars, bruises, and chains, and out of his mind. It's a perfect illustration of lost people in our world.

Next to this filthy demoniac stood the pure Son of God. A broken man filled with the devil is presented in contrast with the One who is a perfect representation of God. Jesus is "Exhibit A" of God's plan for your life. The Lord wants to restore you into the image of Christ. As you look at Jesus and the demoniac, you are faced with a choice. Will you follow God's plan for your future ... or Satan's plan? There are only two roads you can take.

The demoniac lived among the tombs in a graveyard. Don't miss the symbolism. What did Jesus mean when He said, "Follow Me, and let the dead bury their own dead"? (Matthew 8:22). When I first read this passage as a young Christian, I pictured zombies conducting funeral services. I later discovered that Jesus was talking about people who were "dead in trespasses and sins" (Ephesians 2:1). We are all under a death penalty. In one sense, we all live among the dead.

What did the demoniac wear for clothing? Nothing. He was naked. It reminds me of the time I once lived as a hippie up in the mountains. I was trying to find God through nature. In keeping with the hippie culture back then, I didn't always wear clothes. I wanted to be "natural." It felt strange at first, but pretty soon I got used to it since I lived by myself.

Once or twice a week, I would hike into Palm Springs for groceries. I always carried my clothes and, at a certain rock along the trail, I'd stop and put my clothes back on. On one beautiful spring morning I was hiking to town. The flowers were blooming, and I was looking forward to stopping at a local drug store for an ice cream cone. I already had money for my purchase, so I didn't take the regular trail that led to where I would panhandle for money. This trail didn't have the big rock to remind me to stop and put on my clothes.

When I entered the city limits near a church on the edge of town, they were having some type of celebration. On the trail was a young family, a father and mother and two daughters, probably out looking at the spring flowers. When I hiked around a bush on the trail and first saw them, I gave a friendly greeting and kept walking. I completely forgot that I was in my birthday suit.

Suddenly I saw a wave of shock go through the whole family. The two girls' mouths dropped open, and their eyes got big as they instinctively latched on to their father. The wife closed her eyes, and the father took her head and pulled it to his chest and then closed his eyes and turned his head away from me. My initial reaction was to ask myself, "What did they see?" I quickly turned around and searched for what might have startled them. I couldn't find anything. Then I realized I was naked, and I felt so ashamed for offending this family.

I quickly ducked behind the nearest bush on the trail and put my clothes on.

The Bible tells us that, in a spiritual sense, we are all naked. We are just like our first parents, Adam and Eve, who tried to cover their nakedness with fig leaves after they sinned. We all need the robe of Christ's righteousness to cover us. It's what the demoniac in our story needed so desperately.

This naked demoniac had been "cutting himself with stones" (Mark 5:5). When I first read this story, I thought the man was clumsy and fell down and got hurt. But the Bible says he purposefully took sharp stones and cut his flesh. Sometimes people who are emotionally hurting will cut themselves. Self-mutilation is not part of God's plan for our bodies. Did you ever notice that the prophets of Baal on Mount Carmel cut themselves as part of their devil worship? Your body is a temple of the Holy Spirit. The Lord never intended for us to cut or pierce our bodies. The Bible says, "You shall not make any cuttings in your flesh for the dead, nor tattoo any marks on you: I am the LORD" (Leviticus 19:28). This is how far the demoniac had fallen, and it's our same destiny if we never let Christ into our lives.

Coming to Jesus

The most touching verse in this story reads, "When he saw Jesus from afar, he ran and worshiped Him" (Mark 5:6). Don't miss the significance of this sentence. It says that he saw Jesus from "afar." When you picture the demoniac, living in a cemetery, naked, surrounded by pigs, and all alone, could you imagine anyone more hopeless and separated from God?

He was filled with demons. How does a person even become demon possessed? Are you born that way? The apostle Paul tells us, "Do you not know that to whom you present yourselves slaves to obey, you are that one's slaves whom you obey, whether of sin leading to death, or of obedience leading to righteousness?" (Romans 6:16). It was through a series of choices that the demoniac became filled with the devil. It says of him, "No one could bind him, not even with chains" (Mark 5:3).

People who live without restraint are in rebellion against God and His laws. The demoniac made choice after choice after choice until he was far away from the Lord. Yet there was still some small part of his heart that wanted to do what was right. The good news is that he was able to come to Jesus just the way he was—broken, sinful, and even demon possessed.

With whatever freedom was left inside this tortured man, he ran to Jesus and threw himself at the feet of Christ. When he opened his mouth to speak he could not even talk. Even though the demons spoke, Jesus read the glimmer of hope in the man's pleading heart.

When the demons asked to be cast into the pigs up on the mountainside, Jesus said, "Go!" I imagine the man began to convulse as the devils wrestled inside of him like a bunch of cats fighting in a burlap bag. When they were all finally expelled like a violent tornado, the herd of 2,000 swine up on the hillside went berserk. They began grunting wildly, squealing, and then ran off a nearby cliff, bouncing down the rocks and drowning in the water below.

Why would Jesus allow a bunch of demons to enter into a herd of pigs? Just as swine are unclean animals in Scripture, so people who wallow in sin are unclean. It's really a symbol of how the devil and his followers will someday be cast into the lake of fire and destroyed. It was a message that, sadly, fell on deaf ears for the people living in the area.

You can imagine the owners of the pigs, who knew better than to keep unclean animals, were pretty upset. They went all over the region to tell people what had happened. Everyone knew about the demoniac. They used to shudder at night as he roamed their streets shrieking, moaning, and dragging his chains around.

The massive hog suicide left floating pork bodies all over the Sea of Galilee. Since pigs are considered unclean, what happened when all these dead swine were found floating in this large lake used by many Jews? It likely temporarily shut down all fishing since every catch would have been ceremonially unclean. I'm sure the loss of 2,000 pigs also affected the local stock market. Yet Jesus allowed this event to take place because He cared more about people than pigs or the economy. In addition, it served to further broadcast the miracle of how Jesus delivered this man.

Like Mary Magdalene, the demoniac is found sitting at the feet of Jesus. People in the region heard how Christ taught this man. He's an example for each of us to come to church each Sabbath and sit at Jesus' feet. The Bible mentions that the man was clothed after he had listened to the Word of God, words from the mouth of Jesus. Where did he get the clothes? After the demons were evicted from this man and the chains fell from his hands and feet, Jesus led him to the water, where he washed. Then, I believe Jesus took off His own outer garment and covered the man's nakedness, just as He is willing to do for you today.

The story of broken chains is the message of the gospel. Jesus has crossed the span separating heaven and earth and come to the shore of your life. He's inviting you to come to Him, like this demoniac, just as you are—sinful, broken, wounded, naked, and with the chains of sin binding you. Nothing in your life can prevent you from receiving the freedom offered by Christ except you. If He can break the chains of a man filled with thousands of demons, He can set you free from whatever sin controls you. It is His promise, and it is yours for the taking.

The demoniac of Decapolis didn't start off as a Bible hero, but Jesus made him a hero of faith. Will you worship and sit at the feet of Jesus too?

Discussion Questions

1. Why were the disciples afraid of the storm and of the demoniac? Do you often become hopeless in difficult circumstances even though you have the promise of Jesus? Why?

2. What does the demoniac symbolize in this story? (Think about his condition—naked, bleeding from self-inflicted cuts, living among the dead, and chained.) How are you like the demoniac? How are you different? And why?

3. How was the demoniac set free? Have you experienced this same liberation in your life? Explain.

4. Have you ever felt hopelessly chained by sin? How can you find lasting relief from sin and its destructive effects?

5. What do you need to do today to allow Christ to completely set you free? Will you accept His promise that He can do this for you?

Chapter 2
Prison Break!

Bible Hero: Peter

Champion Text: "The Spirit of the Lord is upon Me, because He has anointed Me to preach the gospel to the poor; He has sent Me to heal the brokenhearted, to proclaim liberty to the captives" (Luke 4:18).

Victorious Message: Though you might be locked in a prison house of sin, Jesus came to set every captive free from the bondage of Satan.

———

Harry Houdini is arguably the most famous escape artist of all time. The popular Hungarian-American illusionist and stunt performer would allow others to lock him into "impossible" situations from which he would somehow manage to get free. His repertoire included ropes, handcuffs, chains, jail cells, and straitjackets. In one routine, Houdini was able to get out of a locked, water-filled milk can, but his most popular act was the Chinese Water Torture Cell, from which he was suspended upside down in a locked cabinet made of steel and glass and filled with water.

Houdini never claimed to use supernatural powers to free himself. In fact, he is known for debunking spiritualists, psychics, and mediums. His training in magic helped him to expose frauds that successfully fooled many scientists and academics. His own great escapes were tricks of his trade—hiding a key in his hair, inside a false finger, or in his shoe. Special handcuffs would lock securely when held upright, but snap open when turned upside down.

There are many Scripture stories of people who were locked in prison cells and then set free. But it was not through the use of clever tricks or secretly hidden keys. Freedom came by the miraculous working of God. One story dramatically shows such an escape. It's about a Bible hero named Peter, whose prison break is a microcosm of the story of salvation. Sin has locked all of us in a jail house from which only Jesus can set us free.

The Church Persecuted

After Jesus' resurrection and ascension, the Holy Spirit was poured out on the church, which began to grow astoundingly fast. The Jewish leaders were furious and intent on crushing the growing sect. Indeed, they successfully had Stephen stoned and were grateful for the havoc created by Saul. But shockingly, their best hit man was converted and began preaching to everybody. So the scorned leaders began to lobby the political powers to stop the church.

"Now about that time Herod the king stretched out his hand to harass some from the church. Then he killed James the brother of John with the sword" (Acts 12:1, 2). I believe Herod is a representative of Satan in this story. He is pressured to attack the burgeoning church to ensure uninterrupted power. Pride drove him to cooperate with the religious leaders to persecute the body of Christ.

"And because he saw that it pleased the Jews, he proceeded further to seize Peter also. Now it was during the Days of Unleavened Bread. So when he had arrested him, he put him in prison, and delivered him to four squads of soldiers to keep him, intending to bring him before the people after Passover" (verses 3, 4).

Amazingly, 16 soldiers guarded this unarmed fisherman; his message was perceived as a big threat—and Herod had heard how apostles had escaped from prison once before (Acts 5:19). After marching him through the streets of Jerusalem with much pomp and display, Peter was pushed into the innermost cell of the prison, where two guards shackled him. More guard posts were also stationed to ensure the apostle would not slip from their clutches. Herod was determined to not let Peter get away.

Why did Herod nab this disciple in the first place? Peter was part of the inner circle of an apostolic leadership trio that also included James and John. James was now dead, and John was still quite young to lead the church. It was a strategic move to put Peter on death row. Herod didn't like executing people during religious holidays, so he planned to kill the apostle after the Passover.

The Deliverance

"Peter was therefore kept in prison, but constant prayer was offered to God for him by the church" (Acts 12:5). What was the church doing while Peter was in prison? The Bible describes something more than a one-hour Wednesday night prayer meeting. They were in "constant" prayer, crying out to God on behalf of this beloved church leader.

I am always inspired and encouraged when a group of people pray for me while I'm conducting evangelistic meetings. At times I've actually observed them in a side room while I'm preaching and have sensed God's power. We need more prayer warriors in the church. We need to realize the power that attends God's people when they come together in prayer. And we need to remember to pray for our leaders.

Peter's situation looked hopeless. Let's face it: The church was praying for the impossible. The apostle had 16 guards watching him deep in a prison with even more at the gates. Herod was determined to remove Peter's head. There wasn't going to be a parole or pardon. It was to the king's political advantage to execute this Christian. The church wasn't going to break into the prison and set him free. The odds of bribing guards or slipping him a secret key were pretty much nil.

But don't forget, God loves impossible situations! You might look at some people and think they are so far gone that it's not even worth praying for them anymore. But don't underestimate the power of the Lord. No prison created by the devil is impenetrable to the mighty hand of the One who holds the keys of life and death.

"And when Herod was about to bring him out, that night Peter was sleeping, bound with two chains between two soldiers; and the guards before the door were keeping the prison" (verse 6). I see in this story an allegory that describes God's salvation. We are all like Peter, on death row, destined to lose eternal life. Our situation is hopeless. The devil has us chained by our own sinful choices. There is no way out.

Yet, in Peter's case, we find him sleeping. How can this be? If you knew you were going to be executed the next day, would you be peacefully at rest? Most of us would fitfully toss and turn all night long. Peter was calm because he was converted. His life was in God's hands. Most of the world sleeps on death row because they are oblivious to their situation. They are snoring their way to destruction and don't realize they are under a death penalty. The church needs to pray for these lost people. We should pray that God will wake them up to their true condition.

I love the next part of Peter's story. "Now behold, an angel of the Lord stood by him, and a light shone in the prison; and he struck Peter on the side and raised him up, saying, 'Arise quickly!' And his chains fell off his hands" (v. 7). Who was this "angel of the Lord" that stood by Peter? When I study this title elsewhere in Scripture, I'm convinced it is the angel Gabriel. When this messenger from heaven entered that dark prison, he brought light with him. In our own lost condition, we must have light to see our need for salvation. We do not receive help because we have climbed our way up to heaven. Light from heaven, through Jesus Christ, was brought down to our earth. Truth must illuminate our minds and awaken us so that we see our sinful state.

Did you notice how the angel "struck" Peter to wake him? The angel didn't gently nudge the apostle and whisper, "Peter, it's time to get up." My wife is gentle. When I take a nap and I have an appointment, she will often come in and lovingly tug on my toe and say, "Doug?" That's all it takes to wake me up. The King James says the angel "smote" Peter to get his attention and then helped him up. If you're going to be delivered from the devil's grip, you have to wake up. And sometimes we need more than a nudge.

After striking Peter on the side, the Bible says the angel "raised him up, saying, 'Arise quickly!' " There's a lesson for us in these few important words. The angel didn't help Peter get up all the way but roused him and helped him sit up. Then the angel said, "Arise quickly!" When God is going to break us out of our own prison of sin, there is a sense of urgency. When

God calls to our hearts, He wants us to respond quickly to the gospel invitation.

The Bible says that Peter was chained between two soldiers. So when the angel told him to arise quickly, he could have hesitated. Peter could have argued with Gabriel and said, "I'd like to get up, but I'm still chained to these two guards." If you study all the passages on Peter in the Bible, you'll discover this is one of the rare instances when the otherwise mouthy apostle didn't say anything. It all means that it wasn't anything Peter said that freed him from prison. His escape came only by the grace of God. Peter listened and obeyed, even though he was still in chains. When he acted on God's command, the shackles fell free. Whenever God asks you to do something, in His word is the power to perform. All His biddings contain the strength to obey.

When the angel asked Peter to arise, the disciple did not focus on the chains that bound him. He focused on obeying God's Word. As he made an effort to act on God's command, the shackles popped open and fell off, almost like one of Houdini's mysterious tricks. Except this was no sleight-of-hand. The Lord set Peter free! If you are stuck in Satan's prison house of sin, bound by your own addictions, don't look at the strength of your shackles. Don't argue with God. When the Lord says to get up, we need to get up. When we make an effort to obey, God's power will come over us and help us to respond.

Following God

"Then the angel said to him, 'Gird yourself and tie on your sandals'; and so he did. And he said to him, 'Put on your garment and follow me' " (Acts 12:8). Gabriel told Peter to get dressed. Being undressed is a symbol of our sinful condition without Christ. The message to the church of Laodicea warned that they did not know they were "wretched, miserable, poor, blind, and naked" (Revelation 3:17).

The Bible teaches that following the Lord is a journey for which we must be prepared. When the children of Israel were getting ready to eat the Passover and leave Egypt, they were to partake of the meal "with a belt on your waist, your sandals on your feet, and your staff in your hand" (Exodus 12:11). Peter needed to get dressed. In a sense, he represents us all. Without Christ's righteousness, we are all barefoot and naked. Without the gospel shoes on our feet, we aren't going anywhere!

The angel told Peter, "Follow me." Jesus used those same words when calling several of His disciples. Our responsibility as Christians is to follow God. The angel didn't sit down and show Peter an escape plan. He didn't reveal to him a secret blueprint of the gutter system and suggest they pull up a grate and crawl through tunnels. Gabriel simply said, "Follow me." The reason we end up in the devil's prison is because we don't follow Jesus. When we follow Him, we will be set free.

"So he went out and followed him, and did not know that what was done by the angel was real, but thought he was seeing a vision" (Acts 12:9). In Acts 10, Peter had a vision and believed it was something real rather than a symbol—to kill and eat unclean animals. Now he experienced something real and thought it was a vision. Maybe that's why he didn't say anything this time around!

Completely Set Free

"When they were past the first and the second guard posts, they came to the iron gate that leads to the city, which opened to them of its own accord; and they went out and went down one street, and immediately the angel departed from him" (v. 10).

Peter was miraculously led past several blockades: soldiers, chains, and guard posts. Sixteen soldiers surrounded him. In Scripture the number four symbolizes the directions on a compass. Though we might be surrounded on all sides, God is able to deliver anyone from any situation. Two chains held Peter fast. I think of these two chains as representing the sins of commission (those we purposefully commit) and sins of omission (the good things we neglect to do). Finally, Peter walked past three specific barriers made up of two guard posts and an iron gate. The Bible speaks of three areas of sin and temptation: the lust of the flesh, the lust of the eyes, and the pride of life (1 John 2:16). Just as the angel led Peter all the way out of the prison, so God wants us to be *completely* free from sin.

When Peter and the angel approached the iron gate, it opened without obvious physical force. It's as if Gabriel pulled out a garage door opener and pressed a button. The giant metal gate silently swung open on its hinges. There was no fight. They didn't disarm or attack the guards. The soldiers guarding the gates were completely blind to the escapee.

After walking out of the prison and down a street, Peter's heavenly companion disappeared. "And when Peter had come to himself, he said, 'Now I know for certain that the Lord has sent His angel, and has delivered me from the hand of Herod and from all the expectation of the Jewish people'" (Acts 12:11). Peter suddenly realized that he was not dreaming. An angel from heaven really did lead him out of a top-security prison.

The first thing Peter did when he slipped out of prison was go to the church! There was a gathering of God's people who were praying for his freedom. Prayer breaks the chains of sin and sets us free. Jonah prayed from the belly of a whale and was released. The children of Israel cried to God in their Egyptian bondage and the Lord set them free. Paul and Silas prayed and sang while chained in prison; God shook them free. Even though Peter was asleep in prison, the prayers of God's people worked wonders. We, too, should earnestly pray for others, even though they might be drowsy to the voice of God.

The story concludes with Peter knocking at the door of Mary's house where the church had gathered to pray for him. A girl named Rhoda answered the door and was shocked to see Peter. She left him standing outside while she excitedly ran to tell the others. They didn't believe her until they saw Peter for themselves. He then shared his testimony of God's deliverance.

Acts 12 ends telling about Herod's violent death and says, "But the word of God grew and multiplied" (v. 24). It's a story of reversals, isn't it? Herod is king, and Peter is in prison. Then Peter is freed, and Herod ends up in the grave. Isn't that the message of the everlasting gospel? We who are locked in impossible situations are miraculously freed by the power of God, while the sinister enemy, the devil, will someday be thrown into the lake of fire.

Peter's prison break encapsulates the whole message of the Bible. We have all been imprisoned in different ways. But God promises to send light into the jail cells in which we find ourselves. Truth comes to us through the Word of God, the Bible. When the message to obey strikes your heart, don't hesitate. Get up, get dressed, and follow the Lord. He set a Bible hero named Peter completely free from a prison cell and He will do the same for you.

Discussion Questions

1. Why was Peter thrown into prison? Have you ever been persecuted for your faith? Explain.

2. In what ways does the story of Peter's imprisonment reveal the plan of salvation?

3. What do the numbers of guards and barriers surrounding Peter teach us?

4. How does Peter's response to the angel give us instruction today in our own walk of faith?

5. Just how far did the angel lead Peter out of the prison?

6. Are you presently entrapped by sin? Do you long to be freed from the shackles of any addiction? Will you respond to God's call to rise up quickly and walk forward?

Chapter 3
At Jesus' Feet

Bible Hero: Mary Magdalene

Champion Text: "Therefore I say to you, her sins, which are many, are forgiven, for she loved much. But to whom little is forgiven, the same loves little" (Luke 7:47).

Victorious Message: We become the most devoted servants to Jesus when we love Him with all our hearts.

Monkey trappers in North Africa have a clever method of catching their prey. They fill a variety of hard gourds with nuts and then chain the gourds firmly to a tree. Each has a hole just large enough to allow an unsuspecting monkey to stick its relaxed hand inside the hollowed-out gourd. When a hungry little primate discovers its favorite snacks waiting inside, it quickly grabs a handful of nuts. However, the hole is too small for it to withdraw a bulging, clenched fist. And it doesn't have enough sense to open up its hand and release the tempting treasure in order to escape, so it is easily taken captive.

The tendency to cling tenaciously to tempting treats plagues unsuspecting humans and monkeys alike. The devil traps many people by appealing to our natural greed and carnal appetites, which leads to a spiritual downfall. As long as people hold onto the worldly bait, they cannot escape from Satan's trap. But in this chapter, we'll discover a Bible hero who found freedom from the devil's snares.

Let Go and Let God

We've all heard the tempter's alluring voice urging, "Cling to your sin!" And the Bible is filled with examples of men and women who fell into one of Satan's cleverly laid traps.

One of the most interesting examples in Scripture is Mary Magdalene. Her fame wasn't born out of the traits the world typically associates with greatness. Rather, she occupied a special place among the followers of Jesus because she demonstrated three traits worthy of our notice: a great love, a tenacious loyalty, and a sacrificial devotion.

Before she met the Savior, however, Mary was living a life that was dirty, broken, and helpless. Like the senseless monkey caught in a trap, her bad choices held her firmly in bondage to the evil one. The Bible says Jesus delivered Mary from seven demons (Luke 8:2), and I believe this reveals that the devil waged a long and fierce struggle to maintain control of her heart and mind.

Jesus said, "And if your right hand causes you to sin, cut it off and cast it from you; for it is more profitable for you that one of your members perish, than for your whole body to be cast into hell" (Matthew 5:30). Mary was rescued from bondage because she made a conscious choice to "let go and let God."

Of course, it is impossible to "let God" do anything until we first "let go" of everything and everyone else! That's right. Even other people in our lives must not take priority over our relationship with God. The first and greatest command-ment is to "love the LORD your God with all your heart, with all your soul, with all your mind, and with all your strength" (Mark 12:30). Then, second, we are commanded to "love your neighbor as yourself" (v. 31). Jesus also told His followers, "He who loves father or mother more than Me is not worthy of Me. And he who loves son or daughter more than Me is not worthy of Me" (Matthew 10:37).

The good news is that whoever has the faith to trust God and surrender all for Christ's sake will be abundantly compen-sated—in this life and in the next (Mark 10:29, 30).

It Costs How Much?

Kneeling at Jesus' feet in sacrifice and service, washing His feet with her tears, drying them with her hair, and anointing Him with costly oil, was, in many respects, Mary's finest hour. Jesus immortalized her selfless deed at Simon's feast by declar-ing that "wherever this gospel is preached in the whole world, what this woman has done will also be told as a memorial to her" (Mark 14:9). Similarly, Jesus commended the widow who cast her last two coins into the offering box because she gave everything she had to God (Luke 21:1–4).

It might sound radical or even scary, but to be saved re-quires a total surrender—a complete sacrifice.

And so Mary gave her all to Jesus. She provided for Him not only during His public ministry (Luke 8:2, 3), but she also gave lavishly when she bought the alabaster box of perfume for His anointing.

Mary had overheard Jesus tell the apostles He would be murdered in Jerusalem and rise the third day. Overwhelmed by her deep appreciation for Jesus and all He had done for her, Mary redirected her attention to finding a worthy gift to give the Master while He was still with them. If necessary, she would empty her purse to do so. The money she had saved from her former life and from selling her place in Magdala was a substantial sum, yet it was a constant reminder to her of the wages of sin. Mary determined to spend all of her savings, if necessary, to purchase a noble present as an offering to anoint the Lord.

Many never get to experience the fullness of God's peace and power because they make only a partial surrender to Him. The Lord can fill our vessels only to the extent that we first empty them.

Is the Lord asking you to liquidate 100 percent of your assets and give them as an offering? Not necessarily, but He is asking you to put everything on the altar and then be willing to do whatever He directs you to do. God asks us for a no-strings-attached commitment.

Humble Service

A hospital visitor once saw a nurse tending to the ugly sores of a leprosy patient and said, "I'd never do that, not even for a million dollars!"

The nurse answered, "Neither would I. But I do it for Jesus for nothing."

Genuine love is willing to serve without any remuneration or even recognition.

The world defines success by what kind of car a man drives, what kind of clothes a woman wears, or what kind of house a family owns. With the Lord, it's not what kind of car a man drives; it's what kind of man drives the car. With God, the issue is what kind of woman wears the dress and what kind of family lives in the house. Man looks on the outward appearance, while God looks on the heart (1 Samuel 16:7).

Because all eyes were transfixed on Jesus as He spoke, no one noticed when Mary softly slipped into the room and knelt quietly by the Master's feet. She had been breathless with fear, but now, kneeling at His feet, peace settled over her. She sensed that she was safe under the everlasting wings of the Almighty. Mary silently prayed that Jesus would approve of her deed of love. What the others thought was of no consequence to her.

With loving tenderness, she broke the seal on the alabaster flask and poured the precious oil liberally over Jesus' feet. Jesus did not flinch; He simply paused in His discourse, smiled to acknowledge to Mary that He was aware of her act of service and sacrifice, and then continued His conversation.

As the fragrant oil ran down Jesus' feet, a drop spilled onto the tile floor. Realizing that in her haste she had forgotten to bring a cloth or towel to evenly spread the ointment, Mary removed the shawl covering her head and, without a second thought, released her long, luxuriously rich brown hair from the ties that contained it. Then she began wiping His feet, spreading the oil with her hair.

F. B. Meyer, a Baptist pastor from England, said, "I used to think that God's gifts were on shelves one above the other and that the taller we grew in Christian character, the more easily we should reach them. I find now that God's gifts are on shelves one beneath the other. It is not a question of growing taller but of stooping lower; that we have to go down, always down, to get His best gifts."

The Anointed

In ancient times, Israel's priests and kings were ceremonially anointed with oil as a sign of official appointment to office and as a symbol of God's Spirit and power upon them. Moses anointed Aaron with oil to consecrate him as Israel's first high priest (Leviticus 8:12, 13), and the prophet Elisha commanded his servant to anoint Captain Jehu with oil to seal him as king (2 Kings 9:3).

Thus, when Mary anointed the Lord in Simon's house, it was a gesture of tremendous significance. Just before the cross, Jesus was being sealed as a king, priest, and sacrifice!

Mary was so absorbed in the joy of serving Jesus, however, that she was oblivious to the stunned reactions of the guests seated around the table. After she broke open the alabaster flask, the room quickly filled with a profusion of the costly exotic essence. The conversation in the room quieted to a tense murmur. Even the servants froze, not certain as to what they should do about the unfolding situation.

Mary now felt the piercing stares of all present. Fearing someone might try to prohibit her from completing her mission, she resolutely stood and poured the remaining oil on Jesus' head amid gasps of astonishment. Mary's unmistakable act was the traditional symbol among the Jews for the sealing and anointing of a new king or priest!

The Hebrew word *mashiyach*, which is translated Messiah, and the Greek word *christos*, which is translated Christ, both mean "anointed." Some people have thought that Christ was Jesus' surname, but the word "Christ" is actually a title that means "the anointed one."

Selfishness of Judas

Those who observed Mary's actions at Simon's house criticized her outward actions, especially when she let down her hair. The Bible teaches that a woman's hair is her glory (1 Corinthians 11:15). The visual message inherent in Mary's act of wiping Jesus' feet with her hair was one of humble service, submission, worship, and surrender.

Scripture tells us about two people kissing Jesus. Judas kissed His face in an act of betrayal (Luke 22:48). In contrast, Mary kissed Jesus' feet (Luke 7:38) and then served Him.

The genuine sacrifice and service of Mary was a stinging rebuke to the selfishness of Judas (John 12:3–6). It was immediately after his pious statement of concern for the poor, indirectly criticizing Mary for her deed, that Judas went out and negotiated with his enemies to betray the Savior for the price of a slave.

Judas, indignant, protested under his breath—just loud enough for those seated nearby to hear. "What a tragic waste of money!" he exclaimed. "This oil could have been sold for more than three hundred denarii." Then, as an afterthought to cloak his greedy designs, Judas added, "The proceeds could have been donated to the poor!"

Some of the other disciples nodded in agreement, but what Judas' peers didn't know was that his selfish heart had felt keenly convicted by Mary's liberal generosity. It is often true that those who look down their noses at "sinners" are, like Judas, doing this as a diversionary tactic lest someone should discover their own sin. The most critical and judgmental people are often the ones who are struggling with hidden guilt.

A Public Display

Mary was not ashamed by unabashedly showing her love for Jesus. Too often we are afraid to publicly show our love for the Lord in the workplace or the neighborhood for fear of being ridiculed. But Jesus explained, "For whoever is ashamed of Me and My words, of him the Son of Man will be ashamed when He comes in His own glory, and in His Father's, and of the holy angels" (Luke 9:26).

Because Mary was not afraid to openly demonstrate her loyalty and submission to Jesus, the Lord was likewise willing to defend her in public.

Jesus heard His faithful disciples echo Judas' murmurings. With a sad compassion, He said to them, "Why do you trouble the woman? For she has done a good work for Me. For you have the poor with you always, but Me, you do not have always. For in pouring this fragrant oil on My body, she did it for My burial" (Matthew 26:10–12). This declaration of Jesus' approval brought ecstatic joy to Mary's heart; knowing that the Lord was pleased with her was all she wanted. The weeping woman fell again to her knees and resumed kissing His feet.

Jesus was very protective of Mary because He understood her heart. Throughout Scripture a woman is a symbol of the church, and flawed and defective though she might appear, Jesus is grieved and angered by those who, like Judas, stand by and accuse the symbolic bride of Christ.

Love Gives Lavishly

I know a fairly prosperous businessman whose son was convicted of murder and sentenced to life in prison. The loving father, convinced that his son was innocent, mortgaged his home and sold all of the family's assets to pay the legal fees to get his son another trial.

Even though the conviction stood, the father never regretted the sacrifice. Why did he offer all? Because love gives sacrificially. The ultimate illustration of such love is described in John 3:16. God the Father gave His all when He sent His only Son to die for us.

When Naaman the Syrian was healed of leprosy, his first desire was to express thanks; he wanted to give something to Elisha the prophet (2 Kings 5). His lavish offering of gold, silver, and costly garments was in proportion to his profuse gratitude. Likewise, after Zacchaeus was forgiven by Christ, his immediate response was to give abundantly to others (Luke 19:1–10).

Mary also felt compelled to give back to Jesus because she appreciated how much she had been forgiven. Jesus looked at her, then back at Simon. "Do you see this woman?" He asked. "I entered your house; you gave Me no water for My feet, but she has washed My feet with her tears and wiped them with the hair of her head. You gave Me no kiss, but this woman has not ceased to kiss My feet since the time I came in. You did not anoint My head with oil, but this woman has anointed My feet with fragrant oil. Therefore I say to you, her sins, which are many, are forgiven, for she loved much. But to whom little is forgiven, the same loves little" (Luke 7:44–47).

Mary's total devotion for Jesus, her willingness to be a spectacle that she might honor Him, perhaps qualified her in God's eyes to be the one to first see Jesus alive after the resurrection and the first to bear this good news to others.

When we begin to see how much Jesus suffered and paid for our sins, when we are genuinely converted from our selfish striving for recognition and grasping for earthly gain, then and only then will we be content to humbly serve and to give all to the One who gave all for us, to willingly loosen our fist and let go of sin, just like an unlikely Bible hero named Mary of Magdala.

Discussion Questions

1. Consider where Mary came from and what type of life she once lived. In what way does the life of Mary represent our own lives?

2. Why did Judas criticize Mary's actions? Have you ever done something similar?

3. What message did Jesus have for Simon? What does it mean to you today?

4. Why do you think Mary was so willing to sacrificially serve Christ?

Chapter 4
Rahab's Red Rope

Bible Hero: Rahab

Champion Text: "By faith the walls of Jericho fell down after they were encircled for seven days. By faith the harlot Rahab did not perish with those who did not believe, when she had received the spies with peace" (Hebrews 11:30, 31).

Victorious Message: Even those who were once enemies of God can be saved and used to save others.

When addressing the relationship between faith and works, the apostle James mentions two people: "But do you want to know, O foolish man, that faith without works is dead? Was not Abraham our father justified by works when he offered Isaac his son on the altar? ... Likewise, was not Rahab the harlot also justified by works when she received the messengers and sent them out another way? For as the body without the spirit is dead, so faith without works is dead also" (James 2:20, 21, 25, 26).

No one would be surprised to see James's reference to Abraham, the father of the faithful, but who would think to include Rahab the harlot?

Yet in Hebrews 11, where Paul chronicles the heroes of faith, he writes: "By faith the walls of Jericho fell down after they were encircled for seven days. By faith the harlot Rahab did not perish with those who did not believe, when she had received the spies with peace" (vv. 30, 31).

Only two women are called by name in Hebrews chapter 11—Sarah and the harlot Rahab. Indeed, did you know that Rahab was one of the ancestors of Jesus mentioned in the first chapter of the New Testament? (Matthew 1:5). Furthermore, she was the great-grandmother of King David. Obviously, the story of Rahab deserves our serious consideration!

No Surprise Ambush

"Now Joshua the son of Nun sent out two men ... to spy secretly, saying, 'Go, view the land, especially Jericho'" (Joshua 2:1). Jericho was a crucial city in the conquest of Canaan, and it became the site of a beachhead battle to enter the Promised Land. When Joshua had surveyed Jericho with the 12 spies 38 years earlier, they noticed its massive, menacing walls looming up to heaven, but Joshua was not intimidated.

Jericho was situated near the Jordan, and the Canaanites could plainly see the nearly three million Israelites camped on the plain just across the river. The people in the city understood that their new neighbors intended to dispossess them and reclaim the land God had promised to their ancestors. They had heard how God miraculously delivered them from slavery in Egypt and parted the Red Sea for their escape. They had heard the stories of how the Israelites conquered other pagan nations. At night they could see the glowing pillar of fire rising from the camp of Israel. By day they watched the pillar of cloud hover above the tabernacle, shading the camp from the desert sun while the people gathered the manna that had fallen from heaven the night before.

No wonder the people of Jericho were more than just a little anxious about Israel's presence across the river!

Unwelcome Visitors

Joshua told the spies to go view the land, especially Jericho. "So they went, and came to the house of a harlot named Rahab, and lodged there" (Joshua 2:1).

Now, don't think these spies went on a pleasure-seeking jaunt into the red-light district of Jericho. In these pagan cultures, big houses by the city gates would often serve as the city hotel for traveling caravans. Rahab and her family operated one of these bed-and-breakfast inns right on the wall where wayfaring travelers would pass. Often these establishments had a little extra emphasis on the "bed" available for the right price. That's how Rahab got her title.

So the spies came to Rahab's inn and lodged there. Evidently, perhaps because they dressed a little differently and talked to each other in low tones with a foreign accent, other customers recognized them as Israelites and made a beeline to warn the king. After all, it is hard to hide your glowing countenance when you have lived in the presence of God for 40 years. "And it was told the king of Jericho, saying, 'Behold, men have come here tonight from the children of Israel to search out the country'" (Joshua 2:2). If Joshua is a type of Jesus, then the king of Jericho naturally represents the devil. Take note that the devil knows when God's messengers are invading his domain.

> "So the king of Jericho sent to Rahab, saying, 'Bring out the men who have come to you, who have entered your house, for they have come to search out all the country.'

Then the woman took the two men and hid them. So she said, 'Yes, the men came to me, but I did not know where they were from. And it happened as the gate was being shut, when it was dark, that the men went out. Where the men went I do not know; pursue them quickly, for you may overtake them'" (Joshua 2:3–5).

Rahab's Risk

This is one of the acts for which Rahab is immortalized. Rahab lived in Jericho, and by allying herself with God's people, she was laying her life on the line. What made her do that? Jericho was situated on a main highway at the crossroads of three continents. People from many different religious backgrounds would stop at her hotel, and she would observe their peculiar customs. Yet none of these other religions had impressed her so deeply as the God of the Israelites.

In her heart, Rahab believed that the religion of Jericho was just as foolish and futile as the others of which she'd heard. All of her life she'd been hearing reports about how this nation of slaves had been saved from Egypt and of the hundreds of miracles they'd experienced. Any God who could do such powerful things—and who loves His people that much—was the God Rahab wanted to serve!

I believe Rahab began praying to the God of Israel to spare her and her family from the certain impending judgment on Jericho. When the two spies came through, she believed it was the providential opportunity she had been praying for, and she began to demonstrate her faith by action. It's what we are called to do when we accept Christ as our Savior.

When Rahab realized that her king intended to harm the spies, she found a perfect hiding place for them. "But she had brought them up to the roof and hidden them with the stalks of flax, which she had laid in order on the roof" (Joshua 2:6).

Flax was a plant of which the finer parts were used for making a soft linen cloth. The coarser parts of the plant were woven together into twine, and the twine was eventually braided together into rope. Like many in her day, Rahab probably had a little family business on the roof of dyeing cloth and cord. She specialized in red, or scarlet, just as Lydia was a seller of purple (Acts 16:14).

When the soldiers went out to search for the spies, the city gates were locked (Joshua 2:7). It didn't look as if there was any escape for Joshua's spies; the Canaanites were swarming the city and countryside looking for them. These two Israelites had to trust their deliverance to a pagan prostitute who believed in their God. The Lord often uses humble instruments to do great things.

You might wonder how God could bless Rahab—after all, she lied, and lying is always a sin. However, the Bible record is faithful and records even the failings of God's people. (For instance, we've also seen in 1 Samuel 19:12–17 that David's wife Michal told her father, Saul, that David was sick in bed and, in reality, she had let David out the window to save his life.)

Yes, Rahab was dishonest. She might not have known better at such an early stage in her experience with God. Yet her action came from faith in Him, and the Lord looked on her sincere heart. "Truly, these times of ignorance God overlooked" (Acts 17:30).

In the Bible, a woman represents a church, and Rahab is a symbol of God's church. Have there been times when God's church has been unfaithful? "When the LORD began to speak by Hosea, the LORD said to Hosea: 'Go, take yourself a wife of harlotry and children of harlotry, for the land has committed great harlotry by departing from the LORD'" (Hosea 1:2).

Unfortunately, God's church has a record of sometimes playing the harlot. As a baptized Christian, you are symbolically married to Jesus. You make vows when you commit your life to Him. If you turn from Him and then deliberately follow the temptations of the devil, you are committing a form of spiritual adultery.

The good news is that God can forgive and change someone like Rahab. She ended up being an ancestor of Jesus. And if God can change the hearts of people like Rahab, He can change ours as well.

Making a Covenant

After Rahab diverted the soldiers, she returned to the roof to commune with her refugees. After expressing faith in the God of Israel, she said, "I beg you, swear to me by the LORD, since I have shown you kindness, that you also will show kindness to my father's house, and give me a true token, and spare my father, my mother, my brothers, my sisters, and all that they have, and deliver our lives from death" (verses 12 and 13).

Rahab wasn't concerned just with her own salvation, but also with that of her family. This should be a characteristic of God's church. As soon as we say, "Lord, save me," our next prayer should be, "Lord, save my loved ones."

"So the men answered her, 'Our lives for yours, if none of you tell this business of ours. And it shall be, when the LORD has given us the land, that we will deal kindly and truly with you.' Then she let them down by a rope through the window, for her house was on the city wall; she dwelt on the wall. And she said to them, 'Get to the mountain, lest the pursuers meet you. Hide there three days, until the pursuers have returned. Afterward you may go your way'" (Joshua 2:14–16).

A Visible Sign

What sign would be given to Rahab to assure her safety?

"So the men said to her: 'We will be blameless of this oath of yours which you have made us swear, unless, when we come into the land, you bind this line of scarlet cord in the window through which you let us down, and unless you bring your father, your mother, your brothers, and all your father's household to your own home'" (vv. 17, 18).

What line were they talking about? She had just lowered a red rope out the window, a scarlet cord, with which the men would safely descend from the high window to the ground outside the city. And unless the red rope was hanging from her window when the Israelites came to conquer the city, no one in her house would be saved. The rope by which she delivered the messengers would be the same rope that delivered Rahab and her loved ones. What might this red rope represent?

Read carefully the words of the spies: "So it shall be that whoever goes outside the doors of your house into the street, his blood shall be on his own head, and we will be guiltless. And whoever is with you in the house, his blood shall be on our head if a hand is laid on him" (Joshua 2:19).

Like the Passover blood on the Israelites' doorposts that indicated their trust in God's mercy, the red rope symbolized Rahab's covenant with Joshua through his messengers. This is the story of salvation! It is through faith that we cling to the red rope of Christ's sacrifice for our sins and escape eternal death.

When Joshua and his troops later came to Jericho, they marched around the city 13 times—once each day for six days. On the seventh day they marched around the city seven times. Then they blew the trumpets, shouted, and the walls fell down flat (see Joshua 6).

There were probably many people hiding in their houses when those mighty walls fell. Was it enough to be hiding in a house somewhere to be saved? No. Just as the Israelites needed the blood of the lamb on the doorposts of their homes for the angel of judgment to pass over them, so it was crucial to be in Rahab's house with the red rope in the window when the walls came down.

The spiritual significance of this story is multifaceted. Not only does it tell the story of salvation, but it also has practical application for Christians today. Does it matter if we gather in God's house? Yes! It's very important as we approach the end of time that we do not forsake the assembling of ourselves together and that we attend church. If we do not have enough faith to get us to church once a week, how can we expect to have enough faith to get to heaven?

As soon as Rahab sent off the spies, she didn't delay a moment and bound the scarlet line in her window (Joshua 2:21). She made certain that her salvation was secure before she spread the news to her family.

Now, back to our spies. After three days hiding in the mountains, the two men returned to their camp and reported to Joshua, "Truly the LORD has delivered all the land into our hands, for indeed all the inhabitants of the country are faint-hearted because of us" (Joshua 2:24).

The spies knew they were going to win the battle because the people in Jericho had lost heart. They did not come back and report on Jericho's fortifications, armaments, or soldiers. Instead, they said, "The Lord's going to give Jericho to us because we have faith and they don't." Remember, we are saved by grace through faith alone (Ephesians 2:8). However, if that faith is real, it will be demonstrated by our actions.

Faith for Today and Tomorrow

Let's look ahead a bit further. The Israelites were getting ready to blow the trumpet, the wall was about to fall, and everyone in Jericho was going to be destroyed. Joshua, who represents Christ, had some final words of counsel for them:

> "The city shall be doomed by the LORD to destruction [a representation of the second coming], it and all who are in it. Only Rahab the harlot shall live, she and all who are with her in the house [a symbolism of God's church], because she hid the messengers that we sent" (Joshua 6:17).

When the walls of Jericho fell, there was a mighty shout, trumpets blew, and a great quake shook the earth. It was a deliverance for God's people that the Bible says will be repeated in the future: "For the Lord Himself will descend from heaven with a shout, with the voice of an archangel, and with the trumpet of God. And the dead in Christ will rise first" (1 Thessalonians 4:16).

Those two messengers sent from Joshua represent the Word of God, the law and the prophets. Like the two witnesses in Revelation and the sword with two edges, these two spies represent God's message of salvation found in the New and

Old Testaments: "Thy word have I hid in mine heart, that I might not sin against thee" (Psalm 119:11 KJV).

When Christ was nailed to the cross, a rope of blood flowed from His body. It's only those who have received His Word and are in the body of Christ when Jesus comes back that will be spared that final destruction. Only those who cling by faith to the rope of Christ's righteousness will survive.

Hang On

In 1937, the Germans built an enormous, 804-foot-long airship called the *Hindenburg*. As they were getting ready to maneuver the blimp into the hanger, about 100 men on the ground were hanging onto the zeppelin's ropes. Unexpectedly, the huge airship rose up with tremendous force.

As soon as it lifted, some of the men let go of the ropes, dropped to the ground, and didn't get hurt. Others waited until they were 50 or more feet off the ground before they let go, and when they fell they broke their ankles and legs. A few others panicked and instinctively tightened their grip. They went up with the balloon but couldn't hang on forever. Their arms and hands grew weak, so they let go and fell to their deaths.

Soon the Hindenburg began to hover and drift with the breeze several hundred feet up. Yet one man remained hanging from the airship. The people on the ground wondered how long he could last. They chased the *Hindenburg* for about three hours. Eventually it lost altitude, landed, and the lone man was able to let go and walk away.

The stunned onlookers asked, "How did you hang on for so long?"

He replied, "Once the blimp took off, I tightened my grip. I soon realized that I couldn't hold on forever. So, while hanging on with one arm, I used my free arm to wrap the remaining rope around my waist and then tied a knot. For three hours I just hung there, trusting the rope, and enjoyed the view!"

Rahab's red rope is ultimately a symbol of faith. We must tie a knot in the promises of God and hang on. It is also a symbol of the blood of Christ. We have to tie the rope in our window, then tell our friends and family to get into the house, because Joshua (Jesus the Savior) is coming back soon with an army of angels to deliver those who have stretched out a red rope of faith, just like an unlikely hero named Rahab.

Discussion Questions

1. Why is Rahab renowned for her faith and works in James 2?

2. How does a prostitute, who is considered a Bible hero, give us hope today?

3. What does Rahab's red rope represent in the Christian's life?

4. Why did the spies say to Rahab, "Our lives for yours," and what does it mean to your spiritually?

5. Who was ultimately saved by Rahab's red rope?

6. Why are God's promises crucial to surviving difficult times?

Chapter 5
Washed in the Jordan

Bible Hero: Naaman

Champion Text: "Jesus answered, 'Most assuredly, I say to you, unless one is born of water and the Spirit, he cannot enter the kingdom of God'" (John 3:5).

Victorious Message: The gift of salvation can never be purchased. We are cleansed from sin through accepting Jesus' sacrifice, which leads us to following His Word.

One of the great heroes in the Old Testament was directly referenced by Jesus during His teaching ministry. This is a story rich in symbols and covers every spectrum of the human experience. After telling the people in His hometown of Nazareth that "no prophet is accepted in his own country" (Luke 4:24), Jesus added, "Many lepers were in Israel in the time of Elisha the prophet, and none of them was cleansed except Naaman the Syrian" (v. 27).

Bible heroes are not always from Israel. Sometimes the faith of foreigners is worthy of our attention. This is the case with an exceptional man who was seriously ill and needed divine help.

A Great Leader

Who was Naaman? The story begins, "Now Naaman, commander of the army of the king of Syria, was a great and honorable man in the eyes of his master, because by him the LORD had given victory to Syria. He was also a mighty man of valor" (2 Kings 5:1).

This senior officer was not only famous, but honorable. He was respected by the king of Syria. Indeed, the Scriptures tell us that God even used this "mighty man of valor" for His purposes. Naaman was no weakling. He was strong and courageous and a man with admirable qualities. People looked up to Naaman as someone to follow.

But there was a big caveat. The rest of verse 1 in the King James adds five words that change everything: "But he was a leper." Naaman had everything going for him, but he was dying. It's hard to enjoy the blessings of life when you know you're quickly running out of time. What good is it to gain the whole world yet lose your life?

Leprosy was a deadly skin disease in Bible times that carried a sad social stigma. It was potentially contagious, and sometimes people were quarantined until they either died or were cured. People called it the "finger of God," and it was a symbol for sin. Just as leprosy separated people from each other, so sin separates us from the Giver of life.

A Simple Witness

Next we learn, "And the Syrians had gone out on raids, and had brought back captive a young girl from the land of Israel. She waited on Naaman's wife" (v. 2). It was common in Bible times for marauding bands to cross over the Jordan from Syria into Israel. Raiders would attack ranches and farms, plundering goods and sometimes carrying away children to be sold as slaves.

On one pillaging expedition, a girl was snatched up by a soldier and taken to the market. She was sold to Naaman's wife, who thought she'd make a good household servant. This girl must have assumed her life was over when she was taken to a foreign land and people worshiped strange idols. But God can work any evil thing for good, so perhaps she wiped her tears, remembered how Joseph was also sold into slavery, and concluded, "Maybe the Lord has a purpose for me here."

At some point the servant girl learned of her master's health. "Then she said to her mistress, 'If only my master were with the prophet who is in Samaria! For he would heal him of his leprosy'" (v. 3). She was speaking about the prophet Elisha, a man with a reputation for helping people. It had been a long time since anyone in Israel had been healed of leprosy, yet it seems there was no doubt in her mind what God could do for her master. Oh, that we all had such childlike faith!

A Hebrew girl planted in a Gentile family actually is a symbol of the church. She teaches us how we should let our lights shine in the world. A woman, again, is a prophetic illustration of the church, and God calls us to be light bearers in the world. Keep in mind that this captive maiden was not the only Israelite carried off to a foreign land to be a servant for God. Some of the strongest witnesses in Scripture were among God's people while in captivity. The kings of both Babylon and Persia made proclamations about the God of Israel because of the life of Daniel, a man carried away to a foreign country.

You might feel much like this little girl, carried off into a place surrounded by pagans. Don't be discouraged. The Lord needs representatives living and working among unbelievers. God wants you to let your light shine in the darkness.

Swallowing Pride

What went through Naaman's mind when a servant girl suggested he visit a prophet in Israel? He could have said, "She's merely a child who believes in fairy tales!" But when you're desperate, when all other options have been depleted, it can be easier to believe.

So Naaman went in and told his master, the king of Syria, who said, "Go now, and I will send a letter to the king of Israel" (vs. 4, 5). The king didn't want to lose a valuable general, so he prepared official documents to pave the way. Naaman brought gifts to open the door to receive help (v. 5). He also took a letter addressed to the king of Israel, which stated, "Now be advised, when this letter comes to you, that I have sent Naaman my servant to you, that you may heal him of his leprosy" (v. 6).

Wait a minute! Who was Naaman to go and see? Not the king, according to the girl, but rather the prophet Elisha. Naaman was an army officer accustomed to working with government officials in high places. Evidently, he assumed everything ran through the king. But Naaman's initial contact with the king of Israel ended up being a political disaster. (How would you receive the general of an enemy army that has been beating up your soldiers?) Unfortunately, the Israelite king, a son of Ahab, was not a follower of Jehovah. The letter said nothing about Elisha.

Let's not miss a spiritual lesson found in this interaction. The name Elisha is very much like the name Jesus. Elisha is one of the types of Christ in the Bible. The Hebrew name for Elisha is *El-ashua*. The Hebrew name for Jesus is *Yashua*. The first means "the Lord is Savior" and the second means "Jehovah is Savior." Our salvation doesn't come from mere human beings. Just as Naaman needed to go to Elisha for help, so we all need to go to the Savior for healing. Our only hope is in Jesus.

Proper Channels

Naaman went to the government instead of God. Some people want a political program to solve every human problem, but that often fails. While Naaman followed all the "proper" channels to get help, carrying official documents and money, he didn't follow the Word of God.

Each of us is like Naaman. We all have the leprosy of sin and need our hearts cleansed. Our only hope is to receive the purging forgiveness offered by God. It cannot be purchased. No bribe is sufficient to buy the restoring touch of the Lord. It is impossible to pay for eternal life. We must humbly come to the Lord to have our sins forgiven. Naaman needed to go to God's servant, Elisha, to be healed.

The Bible says, "And it happened, when the king of Israel read the letter, that he tore his clothes and said, 'Am I God, to kill and make alive, that this man sends a man to me to heal him of his leprosy? Therefore please consider, and see how he seeks a quarrel with me'" (v. 7). The king of Israel was insulted. Instead of seeing it as an opportunity to point someone to the God of Israel, the monarch warned, "This man is trying to create an incident and start a war!"

Word of Naaman's visit to the palace traveled quickly. "So it was, when Elisha the man of God heard that the king of Israel had torn his clothes, that he sent to the king, saying, 'Why have you torn your clothes? Please let him come to me, and he shall know that there is a prophet in Israel'" (v. 8). Elisha knew what was happening, so his question, "Why have you torn your clothes?" was a rebuke to the unbelieving ruler. Elisha knew he was called to be a prophet to represent the God of Israel.

The Encounter

"Then Naaman went with his horses and chariot, and he stood at the door of Elisha's house" (v. 9). The wealthy general had brought so many gifts to pay for the services of the prophet that he brought a whole entourage with him—horses, chariots, soldiers, gold, silver, and expensive clothing. He pulled up in front of Elisha's house as he was told and waited for the prophet to come out.

What happened next was hardly a traditional healing service. We might have expected the prophet to come out and pay a pastoral visit that included prayer and perhaps a little oil to anoint the sick man. As a pagan, Naaman probably thought Elisha would come out, have a little fanfare, dance around, throw some gunpowder in a fire, and shout to the gods. That's how the prophets of Baal called for divine intercession in the time of Elijah.

But Elisha didn't even walk out to meet Naaman. Instead, he sent his servant Gehazi with simple instructions. "And Elisha sent a messenger to him, saying, 'Go and wash in the Jordan seven times, and your flesh shall be restored to you, and you shall be clean'" (v. 10). Then Gehazi turned, walked back into the small little house, and shut the door.

Naaman was shocked. "Naaman became furious, and went away and said, 'Indeed, I said to myself, "He will surely come out to me, and stand and call on the name of the Lord his God, and wave his hand over the place, and heal the leprosy"'" (v. 11). Put yourself in Naaman's sandals for a moment. He traveled from a foreign country and got the cold shoulder from the king. Then he brought all these gifts and expected to meet a prophet. But a servant came out and told him to go wash in the Jordan River. It's rather humiliating for a Syrian general to ask an enemy for help.

We likewise might feel it's too embarrassing to humbly come before the Lord and confess our dire situation. If we would be cleansed from the leprosy of sin, we must bow down and admit our need for help outside of ourselves. Our position, social status, bank account, and even church office will not open the door of heaven. Sin separates us from our perfect Father in heaven. Like Naaman, we need an intercessor—Jesus, the sent servant who was our connecting link with the Divine.

A Muddy Bath

Naaman wasn't pleased about taking a bath in the Jordan. "'Are not the Abanah and the Pharpar, the rivers of Damascus, better than all the waters of Israel? Could I not wash in them and be clean?' So he turned and went away in a rage" (v. 12).

If you have ever seen the Jordan River, you'd begin to understand why Naaman was so upset. It's not a colossal river like the Amazon. Actually, it's so small you could easily throw a rock across it. Not only that, it's very muddy. You can't see the bottom. Thus, dunking himself in the Jordan was just too much. Naaman would have rather died with dignity than suffer this humiliation. So he spun his chariots around and headed back home.

Why did Elisha tell Naaman to wash in the Jordan? Did you know the word Jordan means "descending"? It's actually the lowest river in the world, traveling from above sea level to 1,300 feet below, ending in the Dead Sea. The Jordan is a symbol for death, just as baptism symbolizes a spiritual death to our old, self-centered way of living. The Jordan is where John baptized many, including Jesus. It's a river full of meaning for the Christian. If you want to have a new life, if you want to be resurrected, you must go down in order to be raised up.

Through his servant, Elisha tells Naaman, "Go wash in the Jordan." When the general first leaves Elisha's house, he's stomping mad. But God is good because, in order for Naaman to get home, he has to cross the Jordan. Notice once more the role of servants in this story. "And his servants came near and spoke to him, and said, 'My father, if the prophet had told you to do something great, would you not have done it? How much more then, when he says to you, "Wash, and be clean"?'" (v. 13).

Naaman was used to conquering problems in his own strength. We're no different. We all struggle with the desire of self-sufficiency and our salvation. But the way to the heights of heaven comes through bowing low in submission to God. This story repeatedly brings out the role of humble people used by the Lord to help this mighty soldier—an Israelite girl, Elisha's servant, and even his own servants.

A Changed Life

I imagine Naaman stopping at the Jordan; perhaps the horses needed a rest. Maybe while sitting under a tree, he thought of how people back home avoided him. It's possible he wasn't able to hug his wife and children because of his disease. Did he want to live this way for the rest of his life? Through the encouragement of his own servants, he humbled himself and made a decision that would change his life.

"So he went down and dipped seven times in the Jordan, according to the saying of the man of God; and his flesh was restored like the flesh of a little child, and he was clean" (v. 14). Naaman must have been in an advanced stage of leprosy. When his flesh was restored, I believe there were missing pieces on his body that came back, even fingers and toes.

The Bible also states his flesh became like that of "a little child." When Jesus told Nicodemus that he needed to be born again, He was telling him that conversion is like the birth of a new baby. It describes how radically we change when giving ourselves over to God. We become soldiers for Christ with baby skin!

Notice Naaman's response. "And he returned to the man of God, he and all his aides, and came and stood before him; and he said, 'Indeed, now I know that there is no God in all the earth, except in Israel; now therefore, please take a gift from your servant.' But he [Elisha] said, 'As the LORD lives, before whom I stand, I will receive nothing.' And he urged him to take it, but he refused" (vv. 15, 16).

This is how every true believer responds to God's gracious gift of salvation. Born again Christians want to give back to the Lord. They do not give because they are under obligation. They don't return tithes and offerings because they are being taxed. Their gifts come from hearts of gratefulness. God loves cheerful givers.

Naaman's story illustrates for us the process of salvation. The solution for being cleansed from the leprosy of sin is to descend into the Jordan and die to self. You cannot purchase eternal life. It is a free gift. God is calling you to be a hero like Naaman. The Lord invites you to "wash and be clean." You can come to Jesus just as you are. You don't need high government officials or impressive worldly institutions to help. Your position, educational degrees, or money will never free you from your past. Only the blood of Christ can cleanse you from the deadly malady of sin.

Have you given your heart completely to God? Have you followed the example of Jesus and been baptized? If not, I invite you to be like Naaman and descend into the Jordan. Dip into the waters of God's grace and be completely washed from the leprosy of sin.

Discussion Questions

1. Why was Naaman considered great and honorable?

2. What does leprosy represent in the Bible?

3. How did Naaman feel about going to Samaria to receive help for his sickness? Have you ever resisted cleansing from God? Why did you eventually submit?

4. Who were the key people to encourage Naaman to make wise choices? Do you seek out wise counselors when you need wisdom? If not, why?

5. What does Naaman's washing in the Jordan represent to us?

Chapter 6
A Double Portion

Bible Hero: Elisha

Champion Text: "If you then, being evil, know how to give good gifts to your children, how much more will your heavenly Father give the Holy Spirit to those who ask Him!" (Luke 11:13).

Victorious Message: If we earnestly ask the Lord, we may freely receive a double portion of His Spirit to prepare us for the coming of Jesus.

We should all be skeptical about the silly "gas saving" devices on the market today, but there are some interesting suggestions that could actually double your vehicle's mileage. These techniques, called 'hypermiling,' make sense, but most of them are not practical. For instance, you can save on gas if you never drive over 45 mph. That would be a stretch if you had to drive on the freeway to get to work each day. Another tip is to remove the passenger side mirror. It cuts down on wind resistance but also puts you at risk of not seeing vehicles beside you.

Another gas saving tip is to roll up your car windows and shut off the AC. In the winter this would be okay, but it would be challenging when the temperature outside pushes into the 80s! Over-inflating tires by 10 percent could save some on gas mileage, but you'd probably lose dollars by wearing out your tires more quickly. And unloading the spare tire would lighten a vehicle and slightly increase MPG, until you got a flat tire and had to pay for the towing!

Some people claim if you follow many of these gas saving tips, you can increase your mileage by up to 70 percent. But did you know that God has a better plan to give you *double* the spiritual mileage and power that you need in your life?

Chosen by God

"And it came to pass, when the LORD was about to take up Elijah into heaven by a whirlwind, that Elijah went with Elisha from Gilgal" (2 Kings 2:1).

When Elijah ran from Jezebel after his encounter with the prophets of Baal, he fled into the wilderness and ducked into a cave, fearing for his life. But the Lord spoke to the fearful prophet and told him, "Go, return on your way to the Wilderness of Damascus. … And Elisha the son of Shaphat of Abel Meholah you shall anoint as prophet in your place" (1 Kings 19:15, 16). Elijah left the cave and found Elisha plowing a field. When he passed Elisha, he threw his mantle—that is, his robe—on the younger man's shoulders, symbolizing his calling.

Bible names often reveal the character of an individual, and this is true with these two prophets. Elijah means "My God is Jehovah." Elisha is similar and means "My God is Savior." Elisha's name is also much like the name of Jesus, whose name in Hebrew is *Yehoshua*, "Jehovah is Savior." Remember, the angel said to Joseph, "You shall call His name Jesus, for He will *save* His people from their sins" (Matthew 1:21, emphasis supplied).

Staying Close to God

At this time Elisha became the servant of Elijah. The Lord soon told Elijah and the sons of the prophets that he would not die the death of every man but would be taken directly to heaven. He would have a special angelic escort, and he knew of this in advance. The Bible says, "Surely the Lord GOD does nothing, unless He reveals His secret to His servants the prophets" (Amos 3:7).

Before Elijah went to heaven, he was preoccupied with giving final counsel to the sons of the prophets. Samuel established these schools, which were located strategically throughout the northern kingdom. Since Elijah is a type of Christ, we find many parallels between them. Just as Jesus spent 40 days instructing and encouraging His disciples before ascending to heaven after the resurrection, so Elijah taught and encouraged his followers to prepare them to minister without his personal presence.

"Then Elijah said to Elisha, 'Stay here, please, for the LORD has sent me on to Bethel.' But Elisha said, 'As the LORD lives, and as your soul lives, I will not leave you!' So they went down to Bethel" (2 Kings 2:2). Notice Elisha's words: "I will not leave you!" Here is the secret to Elisha's success: He followed his master relentlessly.

Elijah basically told Elisha, "Before I leave, the Lord has sent me on a circuit to visit all the schools of the prophets. You'll probably hear me repeat many things. I hate to put you through this, so why don't you just stay here." Elisha, in essence, responded, "No way. I'm going wherever you go. I'm staying wherever you stay. I will cherish every moment with you. When you're caught up by a band of angels, I want to be there when it happens." Elisha followed Elijah, as it were, to the very gates of heaven.

We need to be just like Elisha. We need to unceasingly follow our Master, Jesus. If we are to receive a double portion of the Spirit in the same way Elisha received it, we must be persistent in going wherever God calls. The Lord wants an army of disciples who have the same spirit and power of Elijah to prepare the world for the return of Christ. Elisha's example is to be our pattern. We, too, will receive strength when we stay close to Jesus.

A Humble Servant

"Now the sons of the prophets who were at Bethel came out to Elisha, and said to him, 'Do you know that the LORD will take away your master from over you today?' And he said, 'Yes, I know; keep silent!'" (v. 3). In other words, they were saying to Elisha, "Do you realize you are no longer going to be an apprentice? You're going to be a prophet in your own right. You're getting promoted!"

But Elisha was not chafing under his work with Elijah. He was delighted to serve his master. His response to the sons of the prophets indicated that he liked being a servant. Some people think serving others isn't glorious work. Not Elisha. One time King Jehoshaphat described Elisha as the one "who poured water on the hands of Elijah" (2 Kings 3:11). This wealthy rancher's son gladly left his lucrative job and inheritance so that he could be in the presence of this mighty man of God.

"Then Elijah said to him, 'Elisha, stay here, please, for the LORD has sent me on to Jericho.' But he said, 'As the LORD lives, and as your soul lives, I will not leave you!' So they came to Jericho" (2 Kings 2:4). Elisha was determined to stay close to Elijah. It reminds me of the difference between Peter and John at the trial of Jesus. John stayed close to Christ; Peter, who eventually denied Jesus, followed at a distance. We need to be determined to stay close to Jesus if we want to be more like Him.

Verse 5 tells us once more the sons of the prophets in Jericho remind Elisha that Elijah will be leaving. Again he tells them he knows and to keep silent. And verse 6 follows the same pattern of Elisha insisting on staying close to Elijah. This last time they headed toward the Jordan, which, again, means "descending." Whether Elijah went up, down, or in a circuitous route, Elisha would not leave him. He would be a humble servant no matter where it took him.

Crossing the Jordan

"And fifty men of the sons of the prophets went and stood facing them at a distance, while the two of them stood by the Jordan. Now Elijah took his mantle, rolled it up, and struck the water; and it was divided this way and that, so that the two of them crossed over on dry ground" (vv. 7, 8).

Elijah removed his outer robe, folded it, and then struck the Jordan. Most of the year the Jordan River has only a little water flowing and is full of stagnating pools and mud. The fact that he had to strike the Jordan in order to cross over implies it was raging during the spring of the year. In the same way that Elijah crossed over the Jordan, from death to eternal life in the springtime of the year, likewise Christ passed from death to life and ascended to heaven during the Passover, or in the springtime. What allowed Elijah to cross over the Jordan? A robe. We, too, may pass from this world of sin to the eternal glories of heaven by the robe of Christ, which represents His pure righteousness.

What did Jesus leave behind at His crucifixion? Only a bloodstained robe. One of His garments was torn up and distributed, just as the gospel would be scattered to the corners of the world. But Christ's seamless robe wasn't torn up. It was too valuable, so they cast lots and one soldier took it home. Jesus gave His robe of righteousness to completely cover the sins of the world, making it possible for us to ascend to heaven, just like Elijah.

I think it is significant to note that Elijah and Elisha crossed over the Jordan on "dry" ground. They didn't get muddy. When they went through the river, they came up on the other side clean. The robe divided the waters and permitted them to go from one side to the other. There's only one way for us to cross over and stand clean before the Lord. It can happen only through Christ's righteousness.

Ask for the Spirit

"And so it was, when they had crossed over, that Elijah said to Elisha, 'Ask! What may I do for you, before I am taken away from you?'" (v. 9). On the last night before Jesus was crucified, He made a similar statement to His disciples. "Until now you have asked nothing in My name. Ask, and you will receive, that your joy may be full" (John 16:24).

Luke provides specific instructions on what Jesus wants us to ask for.

"So I say to you, ask, and it will be given to you; seek, and you will find; knock, and it will be opened to you. For everyone who asks receives, and he who seeks finds, and to him who knocks it will be opened. If a son asks for bread from any father among you, will he give him a stone? Or if he asks for a fish, will he give him a serpent instead of a fish? ... If you then, being evil, know how to give good gifts to your children, how much more will your heavenly Father give the Holy Spirit to those who ask Him!" (Luke 11:9–13).

What would you ask for if you met someone like Elijah? Remember, this is the prophet who prayed that it would not rain and the rain stopped. He prayed for fire to come down from heaven, and it came. Then he prayed for rain, and it rained. What did Elisha ask for? "Please let a double portion of your spirit be upon me" (2 Kings 2:9). He asked for the very thing you and I should request. The Holy Spirit is the greatest need in the church today.

Why did Elisha ask for a double portion? In Deuteronomy 21:17, Moses instructed parents to give their firstborn son a double portion of the father's inheritance. From what we know about Elijah, he was never married nor had any children. And Elisha left his family to serve the Lord and apparently wouldn't receive an inheritance. I believe Elisha looked to Elijah as a father. Basically, Elisha was saying, "My father, I want a double portion of your inheritance." The only thing Elijah had was the Spirit and power of God. Elisha said, "Well, then I'd like a double portion."

"So he said, 'You have asked a hard thing. Nevertheless, if you see me when I am taken from you, it shall be so for you; but if not, it shall not be so'" (v. 10). I think Elijah was pleased when he said, "You've asked a hard thing." God is delighted when we ask great things of Him. Remember how Joshua asked the Lord to make the sun stand still for a whole day?

Suddenly

"Then it happened, as they continued on and talked, that suddenly a chariot of fire appeared with horses of fire, and separated the two of them; and Elijah went up by a whirlwind into heaven" (v. 11). Sometimes we imagine, thanks to Hollywood, that this event was preceded by a drum roll and eerie music. But it took place as they simply were walking along together. Believers might expect a bit of drama in calling upon the Holy Spirit, but here we are reminded that in simple, quiet communion the Lord comes to us. Receiving the Spirit doesn't come through showing up at a special event once in a while with a ticket. It happens through daily time with God.

And remember, when the apostles were filled with the Holy Spirit, it happened suddenly as they prayed together (Acts 2:2–4).

Suddenly a chariot of fire and horses of fire appeared and took Elijah up in a whirlwind. I don't think these were real ponies snorting and galloping down to get him. God's armies of angels are often seen as chariots of fire (see 2 Kings 6:17). This vortex of fire was a tornado of angels that caught Elijah up to heaven. We see the same idea with clouds of angels receiving Christ when He ascended after the resurrection (Acts 1:9) and when He returns the second time (2 Thessalonians 1:7).

The story concludes,

"And Elisha saw it, and he cried out, 'My father, my father, the chariot of Israel and its horsemen!' So he saw him no more. And he took hold of his own clothes and tore them into two pieces. He also took up the mantle of Elijah that had fallen from him, and went back and stood by the bank of the Jordan. Then he took the mantle of Elijah that had fallen from him, and struck the water, and said, 'Where is the LORD God of Elijah?' And when he also had struck the water, it was divided this way and that; and Elisha crossed over" (2 Kings 2:12–14).

Notice Elisha tears his own garments and takes up the robe Elijah left behind when he ascended to heaven. Likewise, we are to lay aside our filthy rags and take up the robe of Jesus' righteousness that He has freely provided.

The story of Elijah is also marked by water and fire. Jesus once said, "Most assuredly, I say to you, unless one is born of water and the Spirit, he cannot enter the kingdom of God" (John 3:5). When you think about the life of Elijah, you see him running down from Mount Carmel through a miraculous rainfall of water. It's as if he was baptized and soaked in this downpour. Now at the end of his life on this earth, he is surrounded by fire as he goes up to heaven. Elijah was born of water and the Spirit before he entered God's kingdom.

Our planet was once baptized in a flood of water during the time of Noah. It washed the world of sin. Someday the earth will be baptized in fire and purified of all wickedness. Then God creates a new heaven and a new earth. If you would ascend to heaven like Elijah, you also must be baptized of water and the Spirit. Like Elisha, our Bible hero in this story, you can ask the Father for a double portion of the Spirit. He is ready and willing to give us this gift. If you have never given your life to Christ and been baptized, now is the time to step into the Jordan. Pass through the waters and then be lifted up by the power of the Spirit. Then you will someday ascend with all God's children in a chariot of angels to our eternal home.

Discussion Questions

1. How did Elisha know that he was chosen by God to succeed Elijah as a prophet?

2. What five important words did Elisha speak that should direct us in our own walk with God?

3. Explain the symbolism of Elijah crossing the Jordan. What does the Jordan represent? What does his mantle illustrate? What did it mean that they passed over on dry ground?

4. Why did Elisha ask for a double portion of Elijah's spirit? What does this mean? Would you be bold enough to ask this of God?

5. What parallels do you see between Elijah's ascension and our own ascension to heaven someday?

6. Have you earnestly asked for the Holy Spirit to be poured out onto your life?

Chapter 7
The Glorious Mount

Bible Heroes: Elijah and Moses

Champion Text: "For we did not follow cunningly devised fables when we made known to you the power and coming of our Lord Jesus Christ, but were eyewitnesses of His majesty" (2 Peter 1:16).

Victorious Message: We can see a glorious revelation of Christ when we study the entire Bible, both the Old and New Testaments.

The brightest manmade light on earth emanates from the top of the Luxor Hotel, a giant pyramid structure in Las Vegas, Nevada. A total of 39 xenon lights, burning at 7,000 watts each and each one as big as a washing machine, shoot a powerful blast of radiant light straight up into the sky. The light beaming from the top of this artificial mountain is so bright that astronauts can see it as they fly overhead. Yet, sadly, this light is totally wasted—it's not illuminating anything as it blazes into empty space.

Did you know there is a story in the Bible that tells of a mountaintop blazing with an even brighter heavenly light? Even though it is seldom addressed, this event, called the

Mount of Transfiguration, or sometimes the Glorious Mount, is one of the most pivotal moments in the New Testament. This monumental experience found in the Gospels of Matthew, Mark, and Luke is full of profound meaning for Christians.

Ascending to the Light

After a long day of teaching and ministering to the multitudes, Christ and His disciples separated from the clamoring crowds. Jesus then said something unusual: "There are some standing here who will not taste death till they see the kingdom of God present with power" (Mark 9:1). It probably seemed to His disciples that Jesus was predicting something really big. But what?

Then, six days after Jesus made this cryptic announcement, they reached the foot of a "high mountain." There He handpicked His trusted "trinity" of apostles—Peter, James, and John—and with them in tow, He left the others in the valley and began the long climb up the steep hill. As the sun was setting, they finally stumbled wearily onto the summit. Jesus immediately knelt and began to pray. At first the disciples attempted to join Him, but exhausted, they soon drifted into a restless sleep.

Then something extraordinary happened! Combining the testimony of Luke and Mark, we're told, "As He prayed, He was transformed before them. The appearance of His face was altered, and His robe became white and glistening. Exceeding white, like snow such as no launderer on earth can whiten them." (See the full account in Luke 9:28–36 and Mark 9:2–9.)

The Reason for the Revelation

Suddenly awakened by the cosmic event, the disciples saw Christ shining with a heavenly light that seemed to be radiating from within. He was not just the humble son of Joseph and Mary, but with unveiled glory, He now appeared as the majestic Creator of the universe.

In the classic book *The Desire of Ages*, the author helps us better understand Jesus' primary reason for this heavenly visitation. In His prayer, "He pleads that they may witness a manifestation of His divinity that will comfort them in the hour of His supreme agony, with the knowledge that He is ... the Son of God and that His shameful death is a part of the plan of redemption."

The loving Father granted them this brief glimpse of His Son's glory, because He knew the disciples were soon to see their master completely humiliated. Their teacher was about to be stripped naked, beaten, and bleeding—appearing helpless and mortal. Just as a little tree stores sap during the bright spring and warm summer to sustain it during the cold, dark winter, so Jesus knew His disciples' faith needed a bright boost on the mountain to see them through the approaching dark day of Calvary.

The disciples also needed this event because they continued to confuse the purpose of the Messiah's mission with the popular Jewish fables of national glory. Jesus knew it was going to be devastating for them to see their hopes for earthly glory punctured by Roman nails, so the Father granted this vision to remind them Christ's kingdom was heavenly and not of this earth.

Why Moses and Elijah?

Along with the glorious light of heaven, the brightest ever seen on earth, two of the greatest heroes of Scripture appeared at the side of Christ. "And Elijah appeared to them with Moses, and they were talking with Jesus" (Mark 9:4).

Someone might ask, why these two? God had also taken Enoch to heaven; why didn't he come along for this special visit? Very simply, these two prominent individuals were living symbols of the Word of God. Moses represents the law, and Elijah represents the prophets. Jesus says in Matthew 5:17, "Do not think that I came to destroy the Law or the Prophets. I did not come to destroy but to fulfill." Moses is the great lawgiver, and Elijah is the greatest of the Old Testament prophets. Throughout the Bible, the Word of God is often portrayed with a dual image. The Ten Commandments were written on two tables of stone. The Word of God is also portrayed as a sword with two edges. Two lamps and two olive trees portray the two sacred divisions of the Bible. But the ultimate testimony of God's Word is Jesus: "In the volume of the book it is written of Me" (Hebrews 10:7). The volume of the book, the Bible, points to Christ, who is the combination of two natures, the human and the divine. Jesus is the Word made flesh (John 1:14).

In Luke 16:31, Jesus concludes His parable of the rich man and Lazarus, "If they do not hear Moses and the prophets, neither will they be persuaded though one rise from the dead." Here Jesus places a high priority on God's Word, and we shouldn't miss it. No matter what miracles you witness, even someone rising from the dead, you should place the plain Word of God on higher ground.

The Ultimate Endorsement

Around election time, politicians begin to campaign and jostle for the support of voters. One common way for them to achieve this is by getting endorsements from as many popular and credible leaders as possible. The Glorious Mount experience is really the ultimate endorsement.

Ever since the time of Abraham, every Jew had been look-ing for the coming Messiah. Several counterfeit christs had ap-peared on the landscape of Hebrew history. Now as a symbol of supreme support, Jesus stood glorified, flanked on the right and left by the two greatest heroes of ancient Israel. Moses and Elijah surrounded Jesus as the ultimate endorsement, to give us a vivid picture that the Word of God authenticates Jesus as the Messiah.

This endorsement from Moses and Elijah represents the highest sanction of the law and the prophets, God's Word, that Jesus is the "Coming One" (Matthew 11:3). They are like the two witnesses in Revelation 11. No other individuals could have offered greater validation for Jesus' ministry than these two giants of Scripture.

The transfiguration is also a direct fulfillment of prophecy. Malachi foretold, "Remember the Law of Moses, My servant, which I commanded him in Horeb for all Israel, with the stat-utes and judgments. Behold, I will send you Elijah the prophet before the coming of the great and dreadful day of the LORD" (4:4, 5). The Word of God is precise. Both Moses and Elijah did appear in New Testament times prior to Jesus' sacrifice to encourage and champion Him.

The Final Word

The Glorious Mount rings with divine authority. Mark 9:7 says, "And a cloud came and overshadowed them." This cloud was actually veiling the glory of the Father, who declares, "This is My beloved Son. Hear Him!" God the Father came to sanc-tion His Son, who received His total approval.

This is important for us to understand. At the beginning of Jesus' ministry, God the Father spoke personally at Christ's baptism in the low Jordan valley and identified Jesus as His

Son. He said, "This is My beloved Son, in whom I am well pleased," announcing that the Jewish nation no longer needed to look for anyone else as the Messiah (Matthew 3:17). Anyone who came before Him was a fraud, and anyone else coming after was a counterfeit. Jesus is the one!

Then at the end of Jesus' ministry, God the Father again identified His divine Son on the mountain, commanding something very simple: "Hear Him." That's a complete sentence, easy to understand. But "hear" means more than just catching audible sounds. It really means "listen with undivided attention and doing." Jesus says, "He who has an ear, let him hear what the Spirit says to the churches" (Revelation 2:17). God the Father, in person, is commanding you and me to listen to Jesus' word and to do it.

There have been a lot of counterfeits, frauds, imposters, and cult leaders trying to impersonate Christ. But God the Father says about Jesus in the Bible, "Hear *Him*." He is the true Word! That's something powerful to contemplate.

Don't Mention It

After the glory dissipated, Christ said something very unusual to the dazed disciples. You and I can barely imagine how these three apostles were feeling "as they came down from the mountain" (Mark 9:9). That incredible event must have been life-changing, and they were probably in spiritual shock, even more than when Christ calmed the storm or walked on water. They might even have been glowing with the lingering residue of light still dissipating from their faces, like Moses was glowing after speaking with God. What doubts about Jesus could they possibly have now? They were probably ready to die for Christ that very moment.

But then Jesus commanded them not to tell anyone of the things they had seen. I imagine that might have been one of the most difficult mandates they ever received. They had just witnessed a glimpse of heaven. They'd seen Moses and Elijah. Like ancient Israel, they'd heard the commanding voice of God reverberating from a mountain, and now they were told not to make any comments regarding this remarkable event. Don't mention it. Keep in mind He was asking three fishermen not to comment on the most exciting experience of their lives. I don't know if I could have done it.

The Tranquilized Church

It is prudent to keep in mind that the Glorious Mount event happened very unexpectedly. The atmosphere surrounding the mountain was quiet and dark. The drowsy disciples were snoozing. Then, BANG! It happened. Christ will come as a thief in the night, when many of His followers are unprepared.

There is a sober warning for us in this experience. At the most pivotal moments of church history, Satan seems to sedate the saints. Just before this revelation of glory, the Scriptures declare the disciples "were heavy with sleep" (Luke 9:32). When Jesus went into Gethsemane, He picked the same three disciples to pray with Him. And they again went to sleep.

So how do we stay awake? Besides the powerful weapon of prayer, we can add the witness of two of the Bible's most extraordinary heroes, Moses and Elijah, the law and the prophets. God's Word can prepare you for anything. Peter refers back to the Glorious Mount, the only time that any of the three disciples write about it. But before Peter's death, he writes passionately, "For [Jesus] received from God the Father honor and glory when such a voice came to Him from the Excellent Glory: 'This is My beloved Son, in whom I am well pleased.'

And we heard this voice which came from heaven when we were with Him on the holy mountain" (2 Peter 1:17, 18).

Yet even after Peter reflects on that defining moment in his life, he adds, "And so we have the prophetic word confirmed, which you do well to heed as a light that shines in a dark place, until the day dawns and the morning star rises in your hearts" (v. 19). Can you imagine saying that after seeing Christ in all His glory, sandwiched between the two greatest Old Testament characters, with the voice of God the Father seared forever into your memory? Yet Peter confesses that however great that experience was, he had something more important, more dependable. God's Word is a light that "shines in a dark place, until the day dawns and the morning star rises in your hearts."

Peter saw Christ glorified. He received a glimpse of heaven. Like Peter, we also can have a taste of the Glorious Mount by reading in our Bibles from the law and the prophets. The two-edged sword of the Old and New Testaments is available to you right now. Open up the Word of God and let the brilliant light of heaven shed its blazing streams of truth into your mind and heart. You will see the true witness of God's lawgiver and His prophet, the heroes Moses and Elijah, and bow down, along with Peter, before the glorified Christ, the genuine Son of God.

Discussion Questions

1. Why was Jesus gloriously revealed on the mountain to Peter, James, and John?

2. What do Moses and Elijah represent in this unusual revelation?

3. Who gave Christ a final affirmation of authority in this event?

4. How might we experience the Glorious Mount in our lives today?

5. Why is the transfiguration of Christ helpful to those who live at the end of time?

Chapter 8
Giant Faith

Bible Heroes: Caleb and Joshua

Champion Text: "Then Caleb quieted the people before Moses, and said, 'Let us go up at once and take possession, for we are well able to overcome it'" (Numbers 13:30).

Victorious Message: God rewards those who exercise great faith in His power to help overcome any obstacles in their path.

―――――――――

Have you ever come right up to the edge of something you'd been looking forward to and then suddenly became terrified to take the last step? I've always dreamed of hang gliding, experiencing flight without an engine, like a bird. A few years ago, a friend took my wife, my son, and me up to the Mount Shasta area, and I finally had a chance to take the big leap.

First, I did a couple of runs off some smaller hills to get a feel for it. My friend told me, "Doug, because you're a pilot, you won't have any problems." Then he took me up to a much larger mountain and put me on the edge of a cliff. After a final check and a few more last-minute tips, he looked at me and said, "Go!"

At that moment, as I stood on the edge of the mountain, I admit to you that I was terrified! Humans don't naturally jump off cliffs. I thought to myself, "All my life I've wanted to go hang gliding. Now is my chance. The wind is just right. My son is watching. Am I going to chicken out?"

My friend noticed my hesitation and said, "Doug, it's not going to get any easier. You just have to decide to quit or jump."

I thought, "I might die doing this. But I'll never forgive myself if I don't try." So, I prayed, "Lord, help me," and I jumped.

It was one of the most thrilling experiences of my life, sort of like being captured by a pterodactyl and carried away. Initially when I took off, I didn't go down. Instead, the wind carried me up. It's as if giant hands picked me up from behind and—whoosh!—lifted me high into the sky.

The children of Israel once came to a "jumping off" point in their journey from Egypt to Canaan, but they were hesitant to take the last step into the Promised Land. They had been miraculously delivered from slavery and were ready to step into freedom. But then they got nervous and thought about everything that could go wrong. So 12 able men were chosen to spy out the country. The names of ten of them have fallen into obscurity. But two of them, Caleb and Joshua, have become Bible heroes. In the face of fear, these two exhibited a giant faith.

Spying Out the Land

Israel's deliverance from Egypt reached its culmination at the edge of the Promised Land. The story is found in Numbers 13, but Deuteronomy 11 gives a few additional insights. The people were nervous about going forward, so they asked Moses if they could send out spies to look over the land. The

Lord granted their wish, and 12 men were chosen to survey the land.

> "Then Moses sent them to spy out the land of Canaan, and said to them, 'Go up this way into the South, and go up to the mountains, and see what the land is like: whether the people who dwell in it are strong or weak, few or many; whether the land they dwell in is good or bad; whether the cities they inhabit are like camps or strongholds; whether the land is rich or poor; and whether there are forests there or not. Be of good courage. And bring some of the fruit of the land.' Now the time was the season of the first ripe grapes" (Numbers 13:17–20).

Moses was saying to them, "If you don't believe in the bountiful land God wants to give us, go check it out. Bring back to the people news of encouragement. Show them what they can expect. They're eating manna every day, so bring back some fresh fruit."

It reminds me of when President Thomas Jefferson commissioned Lewis and Clark to look over the Louisiana Purchase, one of the biggest real estate acquisitions in history. Jefferson wasn't exactly sure what they'd bought, so he sent an expedition to "spy out" the new land. No one knew what to expect. Forty-eight men took an 8,000-mile trip to the Pacific Northwest and back, losing only one man. Before leaving, Jefferson told the explorers to bring back samples of the land, plants, animals, fruits, and minerals.

Likewise, the 12 men who spied out Canaan didn't know what to expect. They didn't have Google maps or photographs to study. Several generations had passed since the time that

Jacob and his sons had lived in that land. No Israelite alive at this time had ever been to the land of promise.

> "So they went up and spied out the land from the Wilderness of Zin as far as Rehob, near the entrance of Hamath. And they went up through the South and came to Hebron; Ahiman, Sheshai, and Talmai, the descendants of Anak, were there. (Now Hebron was built seven years before Zoan in Egypt.) Then they came to the Valley of Eshcol, and there cut down a branch with one cluster of grapes; they carried it between two of them on a pole. They also brought some of the pomegranates and figs. The place was called the Valley of Eshcol, because of the cluster which the men of Israel cut down there. And they returned from spying out the land after forty days" (Numbers 13:21–25).

I wouldn't be surprised to learn that Joshua and Caleb were the two brave ones who carried this enormous cluster of grapes. (The logo for the Israeli tourism industry is a picture of two men carrying a large cluster of grapes, honoring the first two tourists to Canaan.)

Later in the story, the men described the land flowing with milk and honey. Canaan used to be a rich climate with fertile fields and diverse wildlife.

> "For the land which you go to possess is not like the land of Egypt from which you have come, where you sowed your seed and watered it by foot, as a vegetable garden; but the land which you cross over to possess is a land of hills and valleys, which drinks water from the rain of heaven, a land for which the LORD your God cares; the eyes of the LORD your God are always on it, from the beginning of the year to the very end of the

year" (Deuteronomy 11:10–12). God even promised to water this land (v. 14).

The Two Reports

"Now they departed and came back to Moses and Aaron and all the congregation of the children of Israel in the Wilderness of Paran, at Kadesh; they brought back word to them and to all the congregation, and showed them the fruit of the land. Then they told him, and said: 'We went to the land where you sent us. It truly flows with milk and honey, and this is its fruit'" (Numbers 13:26, 27).

I can picture Joshua and Caleb stuffing their pockets with figs, dates, and pomegranates as they went through the land. All they could see were the blessings. When they first crossed the Jordan and saw the beautiful palm trees around Jericho, the other ten saw only the foreboding walls of the city. They didn't believe God had a contingency plan for this doomed stronghold. When they passed near Hebron where the Anakim lived, Caleb must have stopped and stuck his fingers into the rich soil and remarked, "Ah, this is where I'd like to live." And Joshua, near Mount Carmel, saw the place where he wanted to settle.

The reason I think Joshua and Caleb carried the large cluster of grapes back is because they were so excited about what they observed. They had been listening to their fellow spies around the campfire at night. The two knew the other ten were complaining about the obstacles they saw. I imagine that's why Joshua and Caleb ran ahead of the others, tossing giant grapes to their fellow Israelites and shouting, "Look at this! You should have seen the land!" They wanted to first give a positive report of the land.

Eventually the other ten spies slouched back to camp. Doom and gloom were painted on their faces.

"Nevertheless the people who dwell in the land are strong; the cities are fortified and very large; moreover we saw the descendants of Anak there. The Amalekites dwell in the land of the South; the Hittites, the Jebusites, and the Amorites dwell in the mountains; and the Canaanites dwell by the sea and along the banks of the Jordan" (vv. 28, 29).

Joshua and Caleb had shared all the positive news, but now the ten chimed in a negative report. They reported seeing "the descendants of Anak." This was before the time of Goliath, but it was like saying the land was filled with Goliaths. They moaned, "What are we going to do? Can we go back to Egypt?" And the people began to mourn.

We Are Able to Overcome

Caleb immediately responded to this turn in attitude. "Then Caleb quieted the people before Moses, and said, 'Let us go up at once and take possession, for we are well able to overcome it'" (v. 30). He was not about to let this opportunity pass.

Have you ever noticed how many times in Revelation chapters 2 and 3, Jesus said to the churches, "To him who overcomes … to him who overcomes … to him who overcomes"? Why would Christ tell the church that they could overcome unless they really could overcome? It's like those fast food ads that say if you get the right plastic cup with a certain number on the bottom, you'll win a million dollars. Have you ever wondered if anyone ever collects the prize? The company probably counts on a lot of cynical customers who don't even bother to check to see if they have the winning number. That was the attitude of the ten spies. "We just can't do it. Let's not even bother trying."

Some suggest that you can't really overcome sin. Even though the Bible says, "To him who overcomes I will give to eat from the tree of life" (Revelation 2:7), they don't really believe you can have victory over the devil. It creates a lot of cynical church members who are just like the ten spies, listening to a dismal report about salvation. They come to believe, "You can't really overcome. Victory is just a nice slogan and nothing more."

I choose to stand with Caleb. I believe what he preached: "Let us go up at once and take possession, for we are well able to overcome it." Obviously they would not conquer in their own strength, but through the power of God. Listen to his faith! When did he think they could take the land? He said, "Let us go up *at once*" (my emphasis).

Caleb's report of good news was drowned out by strong resistance. The other ten spies shot back, "We are not able to go up against the people, for they are stronger than we" (v. 31). It was true that the seven Canaanite nations had armies that were stronger than the Israelites, at least on paper. The Hebrews had done nothing more than build a wilderness temple since leaving Egypt. They weren't trained for war. From a human perspective it seemed hopeless.

The story of Israel at the borders of the Promised Land describes our day. We are once more on the verge of final events that will usher us into the heavenly Canaan. Once again different voices can be heard in the church. Some are preaching, "We are able to overcome," while others respond, "We are not able to overcome." The latter point at the incredible odds stacked against us. "We were born with a sinful nature that could never overcome." I think the devil is trying to discourage the church today with the same fears. "You cannot become holy. You cannot have a character like Christ's. You cannot cross over. The enemies are too formidable. Just stay in the wilderness."

Whenever I conduct an evangelistic meeting, I always teach the people to sing, "He's able, He's able, I know He's able, I know my Lord is able to carry me through!" It's a simple yet profound and Bible-based message: "I can do all things through Christ who strengthens me" (Philippians 4:13).

We have mixed voices in the Christian world today, just like in the time of Joshua and Caleb. I've talked with other pastors about this. I've personally met some wonderful and godly men and women from other denominations who teach that through the power of God we can be overcomers. Yet for every two people who have affirmed this message, there are ten who have come up to me and said, "Doug, you're preaching legalism. Why are you telling people to keep the Ten Commandments? Nobody can keep the law."

It sounds just like the negative, faithless reports given by the ten spies.

"And they gave the children of Israel a bad report of the land which they had spied out, saying, 'The land through which we have gone as spies is a land that devours its inhabitants, and all the people whom we saw in it are men of great stature. There we saw the giants (the descendants of Anak came from the giants); and we were like grasshoppers in our own sight, and so we were in their sight' " (vv. 32, 33).

Giant Faith

The problem back then, as it is today, is that too many people think like a grasshopper. Yet the truth was that "the inhabitants of the land" were "fainthearted because of you" (Joshua 2:9). The devil wants to intimidate us into thinking we are grasshoppers. But when God's people pray, the devil trembles. He tries to overcome the church with grasshopper thinking, even when the Bible tells us, "Behold what manner of love the Father has bestowed on us, that we should be called children of God" (1 John 3:1). Do you believe this? "Everyone who has this hope in Him purifies himself, just as He is pure" (v. 3).

Real faith does not look at the size of a problem. Real faith looks at the mighty power of God. David saw the giant size of Goliath, but it didn't dictate the size of his faith. This way of thinking is beautifully summarized in Hebrews 11:6: "But without faith it is impossible to please Him, for he who comes to God must believe that He is, and that He is a rewarder of those who diligently seek Him."

The story of Joshua and Caleb ends many years later, when Israel returned after a 40-year detour back into the wilderness. This time God's people trusted in His strength and conquered the land. But there is a sober lesson between these two events. All the Israelites perished in the wilderness because of their lack of faith. Every single Hebrew in that unbelieving congregation fell into sandy graves in the desert, except two people—Joshua and Caleb. Only two men who *believed* they could make it into the Promised Land eventually crossed over the Jordan.

The church today is standing on the brink of the heavenly Canaan. We have a choice to make—overcome or be overcome, cross over or go back into the desert. We can join Caleb and say, "We are well able to overcome," or we can join the ten spies who complained, "We are not able to go up."

Are you facing enormous problems that overwhelm you? Will you exercise the faith God has given you and believe that through Christ all things are possible? Will you take a giant leap of faith and experience a divine hand that will lift you up to heights you've never experienced before? Don't be terrified. God is with you. Take the jump and be a hero.

Discussion Questions

1. Have you ever taken a positive, risk-taking step, and were glad you made the choice to go forward?

2. What positive things did the spies discover? What negative things did some of them see? What would you have focused on in your report?

3. Why did the two spies stand alone against the other ten in their report? Have you ever had to make an unpopular stand for the Lord?

4. How did the congregation respond to the reports? Which report won the day? Do you think the same thing would happen in your church today?

5. What kernel of truth made all the difference in the hearts of Joshua and Caleb? How does this truth impact our Christian walk today?

Chapter 9
The Unsinkable Ship

Bible Hero: Jesus

Champion Text: "But [Jesus] said to them, 'Why are you fearful, O you of little faith?' Then He arose and rebuked the winds and the sea, and there was a great calm" (Matthew 8:26).

Victorious Message: When Christ is in our life, it is as if we stepped into a boat that can never sink.

———

Growing up in Florida, my family lived right on the water and constantly had boats in our backyard, so I've always been fascinated by the sea. I even lived on two different vessels for a period of time—one in the Mediterranean and one in the Caribbean. Since I enjoy scuba diving and exploring wrecks, I have had a special interest in the story of the sinking of the RMS *Titanic*.

Ever since this famous ship sank on April 14, 1912, people have wondered about its exact location. In 1985, Robert Ballard assembled a crew and began to crisscross the north Atlantic where they believed the ship made its fateful descent. Since the coordinates given in the distress call by a new crew on the *Titanic* were incorrect, Ballard enlarged the search zone and patiently studied the ocean floor using a camera on a cable that went down 13,000 feet.

The explorers saw lots of broken phone cables, evidence of underground earthquakes, but no ship. Then one day the camera monitor revealed the image of a ship's boiler. They had carefully studied every nook and cranny of the *Titanic* and immediately recognized that it came from the ill-fated ship. After marking their coordinates, they came back with a special submarine named Alvin to explore and record their findings. Interest in the lost vessel grew and in 1997, James Cameron created the blockbuster movie on the *Titanic*.

In my study of the sinking of the *Titanic*, I've made some discoveries as well. There are many spiritual lessons we can learn from this fateful British passenger liner that sank after colliding with an iceberg during her maiden voyage. As we know from Scripture, without Jesus in your boat, you are headed for a disaster no matter how safe you might feel.

Built the Best

The *Titanic* was built in 1911 in Belfast. It was as long as two football fields and towered 11 stories high. Not only was it colossal, but it had the finest state-of-the-art equipment. The ship had a 15-ton anchor and was driven by three giant props turned by a massive engine that could make it cross the Atlantic in record time.

The *Titanic* was touted as "The Millionaire Special" because some of the richest people in England and America were on her maiden voyage. The ship had barbershops and salons. A grand staircase was made from wood taken from all over the world. It had a gymnasium, card rooms, and even electric lights—which was a first for these ships. The *Titanic* was an elegant and beautiful vessel.

Just before it was launched, media gathered and interviewed the captain. One reporter supposedly asked, "Is it true that this ship is unsinkable?" Though unconfirmed, some believe the captain replied, "God Himself could not sink this ship." One reason people believed it was unsinkable is because it had 16 watertight compartments that were manually and electrically operated. In theory, if a section was punctured, you could seal it off and the ship would be safeguarded.

Captain Edward John Smith was being honored on this, his last voyage, for the White Star Lines. He was planning to retire with a clean record. Never had he had a mishap at sea all of his years guiding ships across the Atlantic. Knowing of the ship's safety features, he wanted to set a speed record and figured that if they had a collision, they would simply limp to a harbor and make repairs.

It reminds me of Solomon's wise warning, "Pride goes before destruction, and a haughty spirit before a fall" (Proverbs 16:18). How often we feel overly confident in ourselves until faced with insurmountable obstacles. It's better to follow the apostle Paul's advice: "Be of the same mind toward one another. Do not set your mind on high things, but associate with the humble. Do not be wise in your own opinion" (Romans 12:16).

Not Paying Attention

Because they were trying to break a record crossing the Atlantic, the *Titanic* crew was not paying attention to some of the messages coming in to the radio room. The operator received several warnings about icebergs, but he was busy transmitting messages on the Marconi wireless (similar to Morse code) from millionaires on the ship who wanted to send greetings to friends in Europe. Wealthy travelers expected first-class service, so Jack Phillips, the wireless operator, felt pressed to send letters and get stock market quotes for them.

Five times he received messages from other ships asking for the *Titanic's* coordinates. Phillips would tap them out quickly, feeling irritated about these interruptions. Then they would reply, "You're making good time. You'd better slow down because there is a field of icebergs up ahead."

Phillips reasoned that the icebergs were far enough ahead that he still had time to care for important business, so when a sixth message came from the *SS Californian* stating that they were going pretty fast toward icebergs, the operator basically wired back and said, "Would you please shut up!" (I'm not sure how you would do that using code.) The *Californian* operator was offended. He was supposed to stay on duty until midnight, but decided at 11:40 PM to call it quits. Just after he turned off his Marconi set and hung up his headphones, the *Titanic* struck an iceberg. Though the *Titanic* had been given many warnings, nobody was listening on the unsinkable ship.

Scripture tells us that intelligent people know how to listen: "A wise man will hear and increase learning, and a man of understanding will attain wise counsel" (Proverbs 1:5). The best counsel comes to us through the Holy Spirit. That's why the most sobering statement in the Bible warns us not to shut out God's Spirit who speaks to our hearts. "Therefore I say to you, every sin and blasphemy will be forgiven men, but the blasphemy against the Spirit will not be forgiven men" (Matthew 12:31).

Slow to Act

Captain Smith was not at the bridge when the *Titanic* struck the iceberg. His assistant, Fredrick Fleet, was in charge. It was quiet at sea, the waters were calm, making it much more difficult to spot icebergs. A crew member in the crow's nest first spotted the iceberg dead ahead. Turning a giant ship is like trying to stop a freight train. By the time the message was relayed from the lookout to the bridge, there was little time to respond. A quick decision needed to be made. Should the ship turn? Should the props be reversed? Thirty seconds passed before any action was taken.

The largest portion of an iceberg is hidden below the surface. It's like the temptations brought to us by the devil. At first it doesn't appear to be that harmful, but then it accomplishes its deadly work. The *Titanic* grazed the side of the iceberg, and its brittle metal was sliced open. A 300-foot gash in her side allowed ocean water to pour inside.

Passengers felt a small lurch when the ship struck the iceberg. Teens on the deck playing a little soccer saw and felt the impact and thought it was a fun adventure. People were dancing in the ballroom to the popular music of the day. Some were sleeping and felt the shudder in the bunks. Men were playing cards in the smoking room and sensed a momentary vibration.

It reminds me of what Jesus once said about His return. People will be busy and distracted by the pleasures of this world and will be completely surprised. "And as it was in the days of Noah, so it will be also in the days of the Son of Man: They ate, they drank, they married wives, they were given in marriage, until the day that Noah entered the ark, and the flood came and destroyed them all" (Luke 17:26, 27).

Captain Smith finally made it to the bridge and began getting messages that water was pouring into hold number one, number two, number three, number four, number five, and spilling over into number six. He quickly called the designer of the ship, Thomas Andrews, who was on board for this maiden voyage. He asked Andrews, "What's the status?"

After doing some quick calculations, Mr. Andrews looked at the captain and soberly reported, "This boat is going to sink. You need to tell the people to abandon ship."

"That's impossible," the captain replied, "this boat is unsinkable."

Because they thought the ship would never sink, they had only 16 lifeboats on board. Not even half of the 3,000 people on the *Titanic* could squeeze into them.

The captain also ordered that a wireless distress signal be sent out. The crew could see the lights of another ship in the distance, but the radio operator had turned off his headset. It's the same with how God sends messages of warning to us. Some people have told the Lord, "Leave me alone. Go away!" The Bible tells us that if we continually turn away from these appeals from the Lord, we will no longer hear them.

A full hour passed before the captain ordered the rockets launched, giving a distress signal to other ships. There was some confusion about which flares to use. Some flares were used for celebration events and others as warning signals. A ship nearby assumed these rockets were not distress signals and ignored them.

No Urgency

Crew members began telling passengers to don life jackets. They were reluctant to tell first class passengers of the emergency, hesitant to create a panic. Even the captain asked the band to keep playing music. People didn't take the announcement seriously. Wealthy people who were used to wearing the finest of clothes didn't want to put on the plain, canvas life preservers. Some never even bothered getting out of bed and perished while attempting to get some sleep.

Many died because there was no sense of urgency in the message given by the crew. The music continued playing, people were laughing, and the bar was still open. Only a small number initially realized the seriousness of the situation and climbed into a lifeboat. These rescue boats could hold 65 people, yet pictures show that some only held 12 people and some were completely empty.

The same lack of urgency will exist before Christ comes. While the church has a responsibility to send out a warning to the world, some pastors don't want to offend people. So they soften their messages. "Yes, Jesus will come someday. But we might be here for a long time." We must tell others that the situation is serious. If there was a fire in the building, you would expect someone to yell, "Fire!"

When the last few lifeboats were lowered into the water, people swarmed to climb aboard, which threatened to capsize them. Some used force to keep people out of their boat. One person held people off with a gun. The last lifeboat actually capsized and only a few were later found, half-frozen and clinging to the keel.

Why didn't people get into the lifeboats earlier? It's a good question for those who hesitate coming into God's church. Why are people afraid to come to Jesus? Because they feel no sense of urgency. "Life is carrying on just fine. Nothing bad is going to happen," they think. That's just what people said in Noah's day. "It's not raining. We have nothing to worry about." People were cozy and warm on the *Titanic*. They were relaxed, listening to music, drinking, and enjoying the luxury of the big ship. Why would they want to climb into a tiny, cold dinghy and possibly get wet?

Like the passengers of the *Titanic* who were called to climb into the lifeboats that would save them, we should immediately respond when God calls us to follow Him. Don't procrastinate!

The Unsinkable Boat

The Bible tells us about another boat that was struck by a storm. The devil tried his best to sink this ship, but it wouldn't go down. Twelve men huddled in fright as the waves tossed them around. Lightning flashed around them, revealing terror in their eyes. But they had nothing to fear, for in that smelly little fishing boat Jesus was sleeping. After an exhausting day of preaching and healing, Christ was asleep in the back of the boat. Not even a terrible storm bothered the peace of the Savior.

When the disciples cried out asking Jesus to save them, the Master stood up, stretched out His hand and said, "Peace, be still!" And the wind and waves obeyed His voice. This ship was unsinkable because Jesus was in the boat. The disciples had already tried to save themselves. They worked hard to row themselves to land, but their efforts were futile. Only in desperation did they remember Christ was in their vessel.

A ship nurse by the name of Violet Jessup was on the *Titanic*'s maiden voyage. She worked for the White Star Line fleet and heroically helped people into lifeboats. A crew member was to be in each boat, so she was urged to climb aboard one and survived the disaster. She was later assigned to another equally large ship called the *Olympic*. Amazingly, it also suffered a calamity at sea and yet she survived. But more incredible is that she was assigned to a third giant ship in the White Star fleet called the *Britannic*. During World War I, it was turned into a hospital ship. It struck a mine and sank, but once more Violet Jessup survived. By all accounts, she was a faithful Christian—and her story is a reminder that no matter how many times the devil tries to sink you, you are safe in God's hands.

It's important to know, because the human race is plowing into the future on a ship that many people think is unsinkable. People are drinking and dancing to the music of the world. An iceberg looms on the horizon, and it will bring the boat down. But there is hope. It's found in a lifeboat with Jesus. He is the ultimate champion of the Bible, the only hero you really need to have in your vessel. As the winds of war, the waves of strife, and the hidden dangers of false teachings blow around you, with Christ as your captain, you will make it safely home.

Discussion Questions

1. Why did people think the *Titanic* was unsinkable? Have you ever felt so confident in something in your Christian walk but it fell through?

2. What types of warnings were ignored by the crew members about impending dangers? What warnings from the Spirit have you resisted, and why?

3. Why do you think people are slow to respond today to the warning signs about the end of time?

4. What other stories in the Bible do you recall about unsinkable ships?

5. Do you have the assurance that Christ is in your boat? Is Jesus the pilot of your life?

Chapter 10
Day of Good News

Bible Heroes: Lepers of Samaria

Champion Text: "Then they said to one another, 'We are not doing right. This day is a day of good news, and we remain silent. If we wait until morning light, some punishment will come upon us. Now therefore, come, let us go and tell the king's household'" (2 Kings 7:9).

Victorious Message: God uses the humble and the weak to share the powerful message of His abundant salvation to those starving for gospel truth.

———

A t the conclusion of World War II in 1945, entire squadrons of Allied planes dropped, by parachute, thousands of containers filled with food and other essentials to the prisoner of war camps holding countless starving inmates. Sadly, some of the emaciated prisoners had become so used to starvation conditions and, not realizing the war was over, hoarded and hid the abundant rations from their fellow former prisoners.

It's hard to imagine being so hungry that you would hide food from starving friends, but that's what happened in a Bible story that turned from great lack to great abundance. It began with a life-crushing siege and ended in unexpected relief. Read carefully, because woven into this story is the message of the gospel.

Desperate Times

"And it happened after this that Ben-Hadad king of Syria gathered all his army, and went up and besieged Samaria. And there was a great famine in Samaria; and indeed they besieged it until a donkey's head was sold for eighty shekels of silver, and one-fourth of a kab of dove droppings for five shekels of silver" (2 Kings 6:24, 25).

During the latter years of Elisha's ministry, the northern kingdom of Israel continued to wander farther away from God. The Lord, in His mercy, permitted hard times to come on His people. Ben-Hadad, the king of Syria, surrounded Samaria, the capital of the northern ten tribes of Israel. His strategy was to not permit anyone to enter or leave the key city and to starve the people into surrender. The situation became so desperate that some had even resorted to cannibalism.

Even though the title of this chapter is "Day of Good News," it does not begin that way. Some parts of this story are so distasteful that I'll spare you the grim details. You can read about it if you like in 2 Kings 6:24–7:20. What's important to keep in mind is how God predicted, as one of the covenant curses, that when His people turned away from Him, some awful things would occur (Deuteronomy 28:53–57).

Sieges were a common way to force an enemy to surrender in Bible times. Some lasted for years. Some were successful, and some failed. Tyre resisted the sieges of many empires but finally fell to Alexander the Great. One of the greatest sieges in Jewish history was the Masada, where 960 Jewish zealots held off Roman troops for three years. Jerusalem fell to Nebuchadnezzar after a two-year siege. Ancient Babylon bragged they could withstand a siege for 20 years since they had plenty of food and water, but we know what happened during Belshazzar's feast.

Starve Until You Surrender

The basic purpose of a siege was to starve the people until they could no longer fight back. With a lack of food and water, the troops would become weak and hopeless. The siege of Samaria reached such an extreme point that people were eating donkey heads and dove droppings. Eventually, they started eating each other. They were desperate to stay alive.

There's a spiritual lesson in this part of the story. When you starve prisoners, you render them helpless. While in the Holocaust museum in Jerusalem, I saw pictures of prisoners who were nothing more than skin and bones. In such a state it took only a handful of Nazi guards to watch over hundreds of prisoners of war. Those who were captured fell into a hopeless state of defeat until they had no fight left within them.

Satan is doing the same thing in the church. He is starving Christians into surrender. Think of how many Bibles are in the homes of our church members but how little those precious books are opened. People are ignorant of the Scriptures because they are not reading their Bibles. Yet they can tell you the entire cast of their favorite TV show or can give you the latest facts about celebrities. Christians receive their strength from the Bible. The Word of God gives them vitality to resist temptation.

Remember that familiar memory verse that says, "Your word I have hidden in my heart" (Psalm 119:11)? Why place

Bible verses in our minds? "That I might not sin against You." Jesus understood the power of Scripture. When Satan tempted Christ, did the Savior quote from the *National Enquirer* or *Reader's Digest*? God's Word wasn't something He carried around in a backpack. Jesus memorized the Bible and hid the Words of Scripture in His heart.

Paul told us, in speaking of putting on the whole armor of God, that "the sword of the Spirit" is "the word of God" (Ephesians 6:17). While the Bible can be used to defend ourselves, it is also an offensive weapon against the devil. We need to spend less time feeding on the donkey heads and dove droppings of the world—can I say it any plainer?—and more time reading our Bibles. It will make us both physically and spiritually stronger.

Devouring One Another

Once again, the siege on Samaria was so severe that people resorted to cannibalism. When the devil besieges the church, keeping us from feeding on the Word of God, we will likewise start to self-destruct. When this dynamic takes place among Christians, when we allow the devil to cut off our heavenly food supply and we settle for anything less than Bible truth, things begin to deteriorate. People stop coming to church, evangelism falls by the wayside, baptisms plummet, and members start devouring each other with unkind words.

You might be surprised at the number of cannibals in your church. Such members will bite and devour each other with gossip and evil surmising. Paul instructs, "For all the law is fulfilled in one word, even in this: 'You shall love your neighbor as yourself'" (Galatians 5:14). Then he warns, "But if you bite and devour one another, beware lest you be consumed by one another!" (verse 15). When church members are starving for the Bread of Life, they are tempted to chew on each other.

One of the best ways to strengthen churches is to involve people in outreach. When a church is only focused on itself, it gets caught up in disputes and schisms. Members argue over minor things and people stop visiting. Outreach helps a church look beyond petty troubles. When people regularly hear the Word preached, they become spiritually strong. Their priorities change, and the mission of the church becomes a priority. Nothing energizes a church like new members who have their first love with Christ.

Unwilling to Die

> "Now there were four leprous men at the entrance of the gate; and they said to one another, 'Why are we sitting here until we die? If we say, "We will enter the city," the famine is in the city, and we shall die there. And if we sit here, we die also. Now therefore, come, let us surrender to the army of the Syrians. If they keep us alive, we shall live; and if they kill us, we shall only die'" (2 Kings 7:3, 4).

What a tragedy. Can you imagine being one of these four hopeless outcasts? Even in the best of times lepers had a tough existence. They were not allowed into the city because they were unclean. So, they'd hang around the city gates, sometimes in colonies, begging for scraps of food. Their disease was considered a scourge from God.

Picture the four miserable lepers, slumped outside the walls of Samaria. The city was encircled by the Syrian army. The soldiers were camped far enough away such that they could not be hit by arrows fired from the city wall. It created a large no-man's-land. The despondent lepers couldn't go inside the city, and they certainly wouldn't have been welcome at the enemy camp. They were trapped and dying. Perhaps there were originally dozens of them. Now there were just four starving souls.

The helpless lepers took stock and realized that inaction meant sure death. If they didn't do something, they would die. They had to get up and move. Sometimes Christians are in the same position: Lukewarm believers are spiritually starving, and unless they get up and take action, they will perish. The lepers knew they couldn't go into the city, so they decided, "What do we have to lose? Let's go visit the enemy camp. Maybe someone will have mercy on us and throw us a stale loaf of bread."

There are fence sitters today who are procrastinating just like these four lepers were. Life-and-death decisions must be made. If nothing is done, they will seal their eternal fate. Many think, "If I just sit around a little longer, circumstances will get better." But the devil works hard to make sure the right moment to draw nearer to God never happens. Those who put off surrendering to Christ might think to themselves, "Someday I *will* turn my heart over to Jesus." But that day will never come until a choice is made to stand up and move ahead. Sometimes it takes a point of desperation for that to happen.

We are all under a death sentence, just like these lepers. Every person on our planet has sinned and we know that "the wages of sin is death" (Romans 6:23). It sounds like a contradiction, but the way to life is through a certain kind of death. Jesus said, "If anyone desires to come after Me, let him deny himself, and take up his cross, and follow Me" (Matthew 16:24). Notice the next verse: "For whoever desires to save his life will lose it, but whoever loses his life for My sake will find it" (verse 25).

The step toward life and freedom by these lepers came when they were willing to risk dying. For them, there was no guarantee that they would find help by standing up and walking toward the Syrian camp. You, too, must stand up and say, "Lord, I am coming to You. To the best of my ability, I will draw near to You. I am willing to lay down my life for You. Have mercy on me." When you do this, you will start to live.

The Enemy Flees

"And they rose at twilight to go to the camp of the Syrians; and when they had come to the outskirts of the Syrian camp, to their surprise no one was there. For the Lord had caused the army of the Syrians to hear the noise of chariots and the noise of horses—the noise of a great army; so they said to one another, 'Look, the king of Israel has hired against us the kings of the Hittites and the kings of the Egyptians to attack us!' Therefore they arose and fled at twilight, and left the camp intact—their tents, their horses, and their donkeys—and they fled for their lives. And when these lepers came to the outskirts of the camp, they went into one tent and ate and drank, and carried from it silver and gold and clothing, and went and hid them; then they came back and entered another tent, and carried some from there also, and went and hid it" (2 Kings 7:5–8).

God performed a stirring miracle—He kicked up the dust on the horizon and created a rumbling sound that caught the Syrian army off guard. These soldiers had become complacent. They knew the Israelites were on the verge of surrender, so they were not ready for battle. But when they heard the sound of an army approaching them, they panicked and fled in such haste that they left everything behind.

When the lepers crept to the outskirts of the Syrian camp at twilight, they were prepared to plead for mercy. Can you picture them limping cautiously toward the enemy, cowering like dogs with their tails between their legs? Would they be suddenly shot through with an arrow? As they came closer, they heard noises from the horses and donkeys left behind.

Finally, one leper crept toward a tent and called out. No one responded, so he slowly pulled back a tent flap and found nobody home. As his eyes adjusted to the darkness inside the tent, he suddenly saw a room filled with everything he'd been longing for these last few years of the siege. Food was piled everywhere. Plus, there was silver, gold, and clothing stacked all around. The Syrians had looted the countryside and were living in luxury while waiting to destroy the city of Samaria. But the lepers could not find a single soldier. The camp was utterly abandoned.

Imagine these starving lepers in rags hitting the jackpot. They began to eat and drink and gather wedges of gold and silver with delirious joy. It's the ultimate rags to riches scenario. Remember, all of this came to them when they determined to surrender. That's how it is for salvation. It costs something to follow Jesus. We must surrender all. But it pays a lot more than it costs. It is tempting to love the world and the things of the world. Yet, when you weigh all the lusts of the flesh, the lusts of the eye, and the pride of life (1 John 2:16) against the riches of God's kingdom, the scales easily tip toward heaven.

We Must Not Be Silent

When the lepers found all of this treasure, they began to haul it off into the hills and bury it. Maybe they thought it was a trap. They didn't want to take any chances, so they planned ahead and stuffed their pockets and scurried off to a hole in the ground or an old tomb outside the city wall to hide their goods.

At some point during the night, however, they came to their senses. These men, who were once the poorest in the city and suddenly became the richest, felt the conviction of the Holy Spirit on their consciences. They were about to become agents of God to share good news. The Lord often uses people from simple and tragic backgrounds. Mary Magdalene did not come from a noble lineage. Jesus came to our earth and was born in a stable. Paul wrote, "For you see your calling, brethren, that not many wise according to the flesh, not many mighty, not many noble, are called" (1 Corinthians 1:26).

It's difficult for some of us to come to our senses. We don't realize the pitiful condition we are in without Christ. Perhaps the sharpest rebuke to the Christian churches in Revelation was directed at the Laodicean church, the church that represents we who live just before Jesus' coming. John shares,

> "Because you say, 'I am rich, have become wealthy, and have need of nothing'—and do not know that you are wretched, miserable, poor, blind, and naked—I counsel you to buy from Me gold refined in the fire, that you may be rich; and white garments, that you may be clothed, that the shame of your nakedness may not be revealed; and anoint your eyes with eye salve, that you may see" (Revelation 3:17, 18).

We are just like those miserable lepers. We need to acknowledge our condition and receive help from Christ. And when we receive special gifts from God, we should not bury our talents like the servant in Jesus' parable.

"Then they said to one another, 'We are not doing right. This day is a day of good news, and we remain silent. If we wait until morning light, some punishment will come upon us. Now therefore, come, let us go and tell the king's household.' So they went and called to the gatekeepers of the city, and told them, saying, 'We went to the Syrian camp, and surprisingly no one was there, not a human sound—only horses and donkeys tied, and the tents intact.' And the gatekeepers called out, and they told it to the king's household inside" (2 Kings 7:9–11).

Did you notice what they said? "This day is a day of good news." The word gospel means "good news." These brave Bible heroes stopped in their tracks. They dropped everything and decided to share the message of God's victory with others. The weakest, poorest, most wretched of all the Israelites became the primary agents for bringing the powerful message of God's love to a city locked in a siege.

You might think that you are in no condition to be a bearer of good news for Jesus. You might feel unworthy to carry the gospel tidings. God can still use you. You might feel you need to grow more in your walk with God before you are ready to witness for Christ. God takes the weakest of the weak to show His glorious power.

I challenge you to share with others what you do know. Humble yourself and ask God to open doors. Pray that the Lord will give you an opportunity in the next day to carry a word for Him to someone starving to hear truth. May each of us come to our senses and, like four brave lepers, tell others about the riches of God's salvation message.

Discussion Questions

1. Have you ever been extremely hungry? How persistent were you in looking for something to eat?

2. How can a person be spiritually starving? Have you ever experienced this starvation in your life?

3. In what ways can people within the church devour each other? Have you seen this in your church or your own life?

4. What did the lepers do that first brought them to the point of being saved from starvation?

5. When we give ourselves to God, what do we lose and what do we gain?

6. Have you become a bearer of good news for the Lord? In what ways?

Chapter 11
The Storm of Jonah

Bible Hero: Jonah

Champion Text: "So they picked up Jonah and threw him into the sea, and the sea ceased from its raging. Then the men feared the Lord exceedingly, and offered a sacrifice to the Lord and took vows" (Jonah 1:15, 16).

Victorious Message: Just as Jonah offered his life to bring calm to a sinking boat full of pagan sailors bound for Tarshish, so Christ gave His life to bring peace to a world of sinners destined to perish forever.

Harrison Okene begged God for a miracle. In turbulent seas 20 miles from the coast of Logos, the Nigerian cook's tugboat flipped over in the middle of the night and then quickly sank 100 feet to the seafloor. In the watery chaos, the 11 other seamen on the boat perished, but Okene somehow found himself trapped in a large pocket of air deep within the capsized vessel.

Providentially, just prior to the accident, God impressed Okene's wife to send him a text message quoting Psalm 54: "Save me, O God, by Your name. ... Behold, God is my helper; the Lord is with those who uphold my life." That became

Okene's prayer. Seventy-two hours later, when Okene was nearly out of air and hope, the water in his soggy chamber began to glow with a green light. A Dutch salvage company had sent divers to the sunken ship expecting to recover only dead bodies. Imagine their shock when Harrison's hand reach down and grabbed one of the divers! The shaken diver shouted through his microphone to the rescue ship, "There's a survivor! He's alive." Nearly out of air and trapped in the cold depths of the ocean for three days, Okene had miraculously survived.

Did you know the Bible talks about another man who was rescued after being trapped in the deep for three days? "Out of the belly of Sheol I cried, and You heard my voice. For You cast me into the deep, into the heart of the seas, and the floods surrounded me" (Jonah 2:2, 3).

The Scripture talks about a reluctant hero named Jonah, who, 2,700 years ago, was trapped within a giant sea creature. He was actually trying to run away from God. A raging storm threatened to capsize the helpless vessel. We're familiar with the big fish that swallowed this reluctant preacher, but sometimes we quickly skip over what happened just before he was tossed overboard. This small Old Testament book reveals how a strange Bible "hero" portrayed the story of salvation in an unusual way.

Jonah Disobeys God

Skeptics question the historicity of the book of Jonah, but Jesus believed in the story of Jonah and the whale. "And while the crowds were thickly gathered together, He began to say, 'This is an evil generation. It seeks a sign, and no sign will be given to it except the sign of Jonah the prophet. For as Jonah became a sign to the Ninevites, so also the Son of Man will be to this generation'" (Luke 11:29, 30). Jonah was not only a sign for that generation. His life is a sign for our day as well. We'll be focusing on the first chapter of the little book that bears his name.

> "Now the word of the LORD came to Jonah the son of Amittai, saying, 'Arise, go to Nineveh, that great city, and cry out against it; for their wickedness has come up before Me.' But Jonah arose to flee to Tarshish from the presence of the LORD. He went down to Joppa, and found a ship going to Tarshish; so he paid the fare, and went down into it, to go with them to Tarshish from the presence of the LORD" (Jonah 1:1–3).

Jonah is not a make-believe hero written up as fiction to entertain ancient people. He was a real person referred to not only by Jesus, but also in 2 Kings 14:25. The tomb of Jonah was believed to be located in Nineveh and was revered by Muslims and Christians who would travel from around the world to visit the site, even in recent years. (In 2014, ISIS destroyed the tomb, calling it idolatrous.) Jonah is an historical character accepted all over the Middle East.

Just as the wickedness of Sodom and Gomorrah came up before God, the city of Nineveh had reached a limit in their sinfulness. Judgment was about to fall. The same thing happened in the days of Noah. God's Spirit had borne with the antediluvians for 120 years. Sometimes people mock those of us who keep preaching the second coming of Christ for 2,000 years, but they don't realize the patience of God, who does not want anyone to perish.

So the Lord called Jonah to warn the people of Nineveh. But he didn't want to go. Have you ever been asked to give a Bible study to another person and felt reluctant to go? For Jonah, it was more than a case of being nervous. Feelings between the Assyrians in Nineveh and the Israelites weren't good. They were constantly at war. Jonah's assignment would be like asking an Israelite today to go into central Gaza and tell Palestinians they are a wicked people. He wouldn't last long in that environment.

So while the Lord had called Jonah to go east, the prophet went west. God said to go by land to Nineveh, but the runaway went to a seaport town named Joppa and booked passage by water to faraway Tarshish, in the opposite direction. Jonah wanted to be as far away from Nineveh as he could get. Tarshish was the furthest destination in the marine world of his time.

Tarshish was the name of one of the sons of Japheth, who was one of Noah's sons. Bible scholars believe he settled in the region of Spain. Some place Tarshish near the Strait of Gibralter near the entrance called the Pillars of Hercules. It was the farthest port the Phoenicians would sail to before heading into the vast and unknown Atlantic Ocean. In other words, Jonah was trying to go to the very ends of the earth to get away from the voice of God that was speaking to his conscience.

Have you ever tried to run away from the Holy Spirit calling to your heart? It's not easy to do because He loves you so much He just can't leave you alone. David understood the relentless love of God toward His lost children. He wrote,

"Where can I go from Your Spirit? Or where can I flee from Your presence? If I ascend into heaven, You are there; if I make my bed in hell, behold, You are there. If I take the wings of the morning, and dwell in the uttermost parts of the sea, even there Your hand shall lead me, and Your right hand shall hold me" (Psalm 139:7–10).

Perhaps Jonah excused his actions, like we all have done, as he ran from God. Maybe he thought, "If there is a ship bound for Tarshish, that will be a sign I'm doing the right thing. If there is room on board for me, then the Lord is leading. If the passage fare equals the amount I have in my pocket, then God must be relieving me of my duties." I can imagine that as everything "fell into place," he prayed for nice weather as he walked onto the boat.

People who don't want to follow the Bible will quiet their consciences with any excuse possible. I've preached to people about the Sabbath truth, for instance, afterwards asking, "Did that make sense?" They will usually agree it did. "Do you believe the Sabbath is biblical?" Once more they'll nod their head yes. Then I'll ask, "Will you keep God's Sabbath?"

That's when the excuses tumble out. "Well, it's just not working out, so it must not be God's will right now." Or they'll say, "I know it's biblical, but I think the Spirit is telling me to stay in my Sunday-keeping church because He has a mission for me there."

The devil will provide you with a thousand reasons not to obey. He even has some limited ability to change your circumstances. He can give you temporary prosperity in order to deceive you. Jonah ran from God, and it appeared everything was going to be smooth sailing. The Bible says Jonah went "down" to Joppa, found a ship, paid the fare, and then went "down" into the boat in order to get away from the "presence of the LORD." Whenever you try to run from God, you will always go down. The Word of the Lord to Jonah was, "Arise." When you follow God's leading, you go up.

Going Down

Jonah went down into the lowest part of the ship as the sailors hoisted up the sails. He found a place among the baggage, got comfortable, and then fell asleep as a gentle breeze rocked the ship. He thought to himself, "Ah, I'm free at last." Then he began to slumber in the sleep of the lost. People today are also sleeping their way to destruction. They are perfectly content with their lost condition, anesthetized by the cares of the world. But of all the people on this ship who should have been awake to the perilous situation, Jonah, the only man aboard who knew God, was snoring in the bottom of a ship heading away from Jehovah.

"But the Lord sent out a great wind on the sea, and there was a mighty tempest on the sea, so that the ship was about to be broken up. Then the mariners were afraid; and every man cried out to his god, and threw the cargo that was in the ship into the sea, to lighten the load. But Jonah had gone down into the lowest parts of the ship, had lain down, and was fast asleep" (Jonah 1:4, 5).

Can you think of another Bible story about a storm-tossed ship that also had frightened sailors who cried out to God for help? There are some interesting parallels between Jonah's experience and that of Jesus and His disciples in a storm on the Sea of Galilee (Mark 4:35–41). The crews in both boats thought they would perish. Both ships were ready to capsize. The tempest was severe. And in both stories we find the one with the answer to the problem fast asleep in the lower part of the boat.

The storm that struck the boat bound for Tarshish must have been quite nasty. Mariners are not easily frightened by the winds and waves of the sea, unless they think they are going to sink. So these pagan sailors cried out to their gods and threw things overboard to lighten the vessel. When you think you are going to die, the things of this world suddenly become meaningless. Remember, Jesus said, "For what profit is it to a man if he gains the whole world, and loses his own soul?" (Matthew 16:26).

Many people journey through this world for the one purpose of making money. Each day is consumed with filling their ship with more belongings. But Christ warned, "Take heed and beware of covetousness, for one's life does not consist in the abundance of the things he possesses" (Luke 12:15). We live in a generation of people who possess more material goods than any other generation in the history of the world.

More of us would be happier if we copied the sailors in this story and threw away (or sold) many of the things bulging out of our closets and crammed in our garages and storage units. Some people are so occupied with their belongings that they can hardly leave home and come to church for fear that a burglar will rob them. We should spend more time with our families and with the Lord than with oiling, watering, repairing, upgrading, polishing, and guarding our worldly goods.

The captain of the ship eventually discovered Jonah. He didn't even know the name of the wayward prophet. "So the captain came to him, and said to him, 'What do you mean, sleeper? Arise, call on your God; perhaps your God will consider us, so that we may not perish'" (Jonah 1:6). He was quite indignant. "What is this? Our ship is about to go down and you're asleep? Get up and pray!" It almost sounds like a revival sermon, doesn't it? Remember Jesus' words that Jonah would be a sign for an evil generation? The experience of Jonah, like the ten sleeping virgins in Jesus' parable, is a call to our generation to wake up spiritually. We are on the verge of Christ's return. We need to spend much more time in earnest prayer or we'll perish.

The only person in the boat bound for Tarshish who knew the Lord was Jonah. He had the answer to their problem. The only person in the disciples' storm-tossed boat who had the solution to their sinking ship was Jesus. He was the answer to their predicament and to all of ours as well. We need to cry out for help just like those desperate sailors and disciples.

Jonah finally came up on deck. The sailors were now frantic.

> "They said to one another, 'Come, let us cast lots, that we may know for whose cause this trouble has come upon us.' So they cast lots, and the lot fell on Jonah. Then they said to him, 'Please tell us! For whose cause is this trouble upon us? What is your occupation? And where do you come from? What is your country? And of what people are you?' So he said to them, 'I am a Hebrew; and I fear the LORD, the God of heaven, who made the sea and the dry land'" (Jonah 1:7–9).

The only passenger on this ship full of pagans, who knew the true reason for the storm, was Jonah. Nobody was interested in taking Bible studies from this reluctant missionary at the beginning of the trip, but now he had everyone's attention. Have you noticed that your friends and neighbors might not be interested in your faith when life is going well, but when tragedy strikes they are suddenly open? I have neighbors who have been my friends for years. They have not been open to hearing about the gospel from their "preacher" neighbor until major difficulties have come to them. Storms have a way of focusing our attention.

The Sacrifice

Here is how the men responded to Jonah during the gale:

"Then the men were exceedingly afraid, and said to him, 'Why have you done this?' For the men knew that he fled from the presence of the LORD, because he had told them. Then they said to him, 'What shall we do to you that the sea may be calm for us?'—for the sea was growing more tempestuous. And he said to them, 'Pick me up and throw me into the sea; then the sea will become calm for you. For I know that this great tempest is because of me.' Nevertheless the men rowed hard to return to land, but they could not, for the sea continued to grow more tempestuous against them. Therefore they cried out to the LORD and said, 'We pray, O LORD, please do not let us perish for this man's life, and do not charge us with innocent blood; for You, O LORD, have done as it pleased You'" (Jonah 1:10–14).

Now comes a critical point in the story. "So they picked up Jonah and threw him into the sea, and the sea ceased from its raging. Then the men feared the LORD exceedingly, and offered a sacrifice to the LORD and took vows" (verses 15, 16).

Why didn't Jonah just take a running leap over the railing of the ship? Why did he ask the men to throw him overboard? Why were they part of this sacrificial offering? This terrible storm had brought them to a place of absolute surrender. They had thrown everything overboard the ship and cried out to their pagan gods. Finally they were willing to sacrifice the life of a person in order to be saved. If you listen carefully, you will hear the gospel story in this message that is to be a sign for our generation.

We, too, must come to a place of absolute surrender if we would be saved. We must be willing to not only sacrifice all, but take responsibility for the death of Jesus. Our sins make us culpable. In truth, each of us has crucified Christ. Our wrong deeds have driven nails into those loving hands. Our transgressions bruised the back of the Son of God and eventually swallowed Him up in death. If the raging storm of sin in our lives is ever going to stop, we must bear the liability for the sacrifice of the Lamb of God.

When Jonah was thrown into the sea, the turbulent waters became calm. Like Jonah, we must be willing to sacrifice self if we would experience God's peace. Paul said, "I have been crucified with Christ; it is no longer I who live, but Christ lives in me" (Galatians 2:20). Jesus explained, "For whoever desires to save his life will lose it, but whoever loses his life for My sake will find it" (Matthew 16:25). In one sense, Jonah died when he sank into the sea and was miraculously resurrected when the fish cast him on the shore after three days. Jesus was also in the grave for three days and then came back to life. Likewise, we may experience the resurrection of life when we cast ourselves down at the foot of the cross.

Though Jonah was a stubborn missionary, he is still a Bible hero who teaches us to surrender to God in order to find true rest. Jonah's name means "dove," which is often used as a symbol of peace. If you are experiencing tempests that threaten to overwhelm you, follow the example of Jonah, a reluctant prophet who ran from God. Surrender yourself into the hands of the Lord. He will bear you up through any trial, even when you feel like you are sinking to the bottom of the sea.

Discussion Questions

1. What other stories in the Bible can you recall that tell about boats in storms? Which one is most meaningful to you and why?

2. Why did Jonah try to run away from God? Have you ever done the same in your life?

3. How did the sailors respond to the storm? How would you have responded?

4. In what way is the church today like Jonah?

5. In being thrown overboard, how was Jonah a symbol for Christ?

6. Have you come to a point in your life where you are willing to surrender all for Jesus? If not, would you be willing to take that step right now?

Other Resources

 ISHEAVENFORREAL.COM

 **BIBLEHISTORY**.COM

 TENCOMMANDMENTFACTS.COM

 **HELLTRUTH**.COM

 TRUTHABOUTDEATH.COM

 **GHOSTTRUTH**.COM

 SABBATHTRUTH.COM

 **BIBLEUNIVERSE**.COM

 BIBLEPROPHECYTRUTH.COM

 **666TRUTH**.ORG